EVENT-DRIVEN BUSINESS SOLUTIONS
Today's Revolution In Business and Information Technology

Eric L. Denna
Warnick/Deloitte & Touche Faculty Fellow
School of Accountancy and Information Systems
Brigham Young University

J. Owen Cherrington
Director, Information Systems Group
School of Accountancy and Information Systems
Brigham Young University

David P. Andros
IBM Director
Office of the Controller
IBM Corporation

Anita Sawyer Hollander
Associate Professor
Department of Accounting
Florida State University

BUSINESS ONE IRWIN
Homewood, IL 60430

This publication is designed to provide accurate and authoritative information in regard to the subject matter covered. It is sold with the understanding that neither the author nor the publisher is engaged in rendering legal, accounting, or other professional service. If legal advice or other expert assistance is required, the services of a competent professional person should be sought.

From a Declaration of Principles jointly adopted by a Committee of the American Bar Association and a Committee of Publishers.

Sponsoring editor:	Mike Desposito
Project editor:	Jane Lightell
Production manager:	Ann Cassady
Typeface:	11/13 Times Roman
Printer:	Arcata Graphics/Kingsport

Library of Congress Cataloging-in-Publication Data

Event-driven business solutions : today's revolution in business and

information technology / Eric L. Denna . . . [et al.].

p.   cm.

Includes bibliographical references.

ISBN 1-55623-942-4

1. Management—Communication systems.   2. Information technology.

I. Denna, Eric L.

HD30.335.E94   1993

658.4'5—dc20   93-1266

Printed in the United States of America

To our families

We would be far less without their love and support. We especially remember Oleta Andros whose passing occured just before the book was printed. We wish she could have seen this effort to its end and that we could have enjoyed her approving smile.

Preface

In his book *The Prince*, Machievelli declared:

> It must be considered that there is nothing more difficult to carry out, nor more doubtful of success, nor more dangerous to handle than to initiate a new order of things. For the reformer has enemies in all those who profit by the old order, and only lukewarm defenders by all those who could profit by the new order. This lukewarmness arises partly from fear of their adversaries who have the laws in their favor, and partly from the incredulity of mankind who do not truly believe in anything new until they have had actual experience with it.[1]

This quote is an appropriate introduction to this book because throughout it we call for a new order of things. We believe the changes we call for result in substantial increases in value to individuals, organizations, and society as a whole. Our call for change is in answer to the demands of today's challenging business world. The need for change has reached a critical stage throughout the world. Therefore, we have tried to make sure the concepts in this book are applicable in emerging and well-established economies, all of which are grappling with our new world. In fact, we have presented these concepts in many places throughout the world to leaders in business, education, and government. Without exception, the discussions have been stimulating, enlightening, and often controversial. The results have always led to some kind of improvement.

To distinguish ourselves from others who have thrown rocks at business, accounting, and IT professionals, we offer proven concepts to respond to our challenging times. Although three of us spend most of our time in the proverbial "ivory tower," an unlikely source for practical solutions, David Andros has managed to make sure this book presents concepts that are either actually proven in the furnace of application, or reasonable suggestions worthy of consideration.

This book is not intended to provide an encyclopedic reference of either traditional business systems or event-driven business solutions. Our purpose is to change the way people think about business processes, organization

---

[1]N. Machiavelli, *The Prince*. Translated by Luigi Rice, Rev. E. R. P. Vincent (New York: New American Library, 1952) p. 10.

structures, the use of technology and business measurements, and to consider the potential role and contribution of what we call business solution professionals. We see a large gap between the skills needed to solve business problems and what is taught today in our colleges and universities. We hope the material presented in this book has value in defining the nature of business solutions needed today and the skills of new business solution professionals. If our thoughts strike a harmonious chord with you, we hope you will make your views known to educators. The first question organizations ask us after choosing to adopt the principles of this book is, "Where can I find people trained in this kind of thinking and skills?" Unfortunately, the list is not very long. We hope this book, along with your involvement, helps make the list of trained professionals longer by encouraging and guiding changes in educating business solution professionals. Enjoy!

Eric L. Denna
J. Owen Cherrington
David P. Andros
Anita Sawyer Hollander

Acknowledgments

We are indebted to Rick Roth and Jeff Gibbs of Price Waterhouse; Eileen Browne and Rob Clarke of the Office of Financial Management for the State of Washington; Jay Smith and Marshall Romney of Brigham Young University; Dave Burta of AMS; and Silvio Lanaro of IBM. Special recognition goes to Sue Andrulis and Jeanine Cotter of IBM for their late nights and long weekends spent in reviewing several "rough" drafts as we approached a publishable version. All of these people have provided valuable criticisms and insightful suggestions regarding the content of the book.

We are also very indebted to Nina Whitehead who took on the task of providing camera ready copy for printing the book. As if challenging a variety of business, technical, and professional paradigms was not enough, we tackled the traditional paradigm of publishing a book as well. We could not have done so without Nina's professionalism, meticulousness, and speed. She never ceases to amaze us. We hope she will continue to work with us in the future.

Most importantly, we wish to give special thanks to Bill McCarthy, whose creativity and ingenuity have provided a significant theoretical foundation for the concepts of this book. Therefore, Bill's influence reaches far beyond the few specific references to which he is credited. Unfortunately, society does not recognize the contribution of truly brilliant people in a very timely manner. We hope this work escalates the belated recognition Bill deserves for being a scholar well ahead of his time.

Table of Contents

Chapter One

Today's Business Challenge and Tomorrow's Opportunity
What Are the Problems, Opportunities, and Solutions?

WELCOME TO THE NEW WORLD!

Today's business world is quite different from what it was even five short years ago. We continue to see dramatic changes in the size and structure of organizations and in the goods and services offered. Competition is changing as a result of an increasingly global marketplace. The risks organizations face due to liability, fraud, or good old honest mistakes are far more prevalent and significant. Tremendous diversity exists in the types of information needed to effectively manage business processes in this new world. Furthermore, we are living amid tremendous technological change.

Futurist Alvin Toffler concludes that this new world:

> challenges all our old assumptions. Old ways of thinking, old formulas, dogmas, and ideologies, no matter how cherished or how useful in the past, no longer fit the facts. The world that is fast emerging from the clash of new values and technologies, new geopolitical relationships, new life-styles and modes of communication, demands wholly new ideas and analogies, classifications and concepts. We cannot cram the embryonic world of tomorrow into yesterday's conventional cubbyholes. Nor are the orthodox attitudes or moods appropriate.[1]

Some have compared running an organization today to flying an F-15 into battle. In battle, pilots must:

Make timely and effective decisions

---

[1]A. Toffler, *The Third Wave*, (New York: Bantam Books, 1990), p. 2.

1

Constantly make course corrections to meet mission objectives as effectively and efficiently as possible

Control risk by developing, maintaining, and adhering to an effective set of procedures.

Pilots use two key resources to perform their responsibilities: a navigator and the information and control system. The navigator uses the information system to constantly feed pilots information to aid them in discharging their responsibilities. Pilots use this same system to implement decisions to effect changes in direction or address risks that arise while working to achieve an objective. Without an effective navigator and system there is little hope of surviving a flight, let alone achieving any meaningful objectives. The same is true in business. Unless businesspeople have an effective navigator and a system which supports timely decision making, facilitates constant course corrections, and helps control risk in real time, organizations are far less likely to survive, let alone achieve any meaningful objectives.

Unfortunately, the architecture and function of traditional business systems and the roles of business and information technology (IT) professionals do not match the sophistication or responsiveness of the navigators and systems supporting F-15 pilots. These traditional systems tend to cripple both business people and support personnel attempting to negotiate an organization through today's business environment by not supporting timely decision making, changes in course, or control of risk. In addition, traditional business systems that provide an organization with its traditional measurements of success may no longer accurately reflect the achievement of its objectives.

While there are many business systems in place today that provide measurements, the most prevalent, and in many instances, the only measurement system is the accounting system. Focusing only on financial performance, accounting systems fall short in providing the measurements for today's world.

As evidence of this crisis, Bob Elliott, partner at the national office of KPMG/Peat Marwick, recently quoted a CEO friend who said:

> Trying to run my company with the output of the accounting department is like trying to fly an airplane with only one gauge on the instrument panel — and that gauge tells me the sum of airspeed and altitude. If it's low, I'm in trouble, but I don't even know why![2]

---

[2]R. Elliott, "U.S. Accounting: A National Emergency," *Financial Reporting and Standard Setting*, American Institute of Certified Public Accountants, 1991, p. 21.

Elliott's CEO friend is not alone. Today's accounting system is being sharply criticized by regulators, legislators, the legal community, educators, and society in general. For example, Robert Eccles, at The Harvard Business School, recently observed:

> For years, senior executives in a broad range of industries have been rethinking how to measure the performance of their businesses. They have recognized that new strategies and competitive realities demand new measurement systems. Now they are deeply engaged in defining and developing those systems for their companies. At the heart of this revolution lies a radical decision: to shift from treating financial figures as the foundation for performance measurement to treating them as one among a broader set of measures.... The ranks of companies enlisting in this revolution are rising daily. Senior managers at one large, high-tech manufacturer recently took direct responsibility for adding customer satisfaction, quality, market share, and human resources to their formal measurement system. The impetus was their realization that the company's existing system, which was largely financial, undercut its strategy, which focused on customer service. At a smaller manufacturer, the catalyst was a leveraged recapitalization that gave the CEO the opportunity formally to reorder the company's priorities. On the new list, earnings per share dropped to last place, preceded by customer satisfaction, cash flow, manufacturing effectiveness, and innovation (in that order). On the old list, earnings per share stood first and almost alone.[3]

Lest you think things are any better outside accounting, business systems in general tend to simply perpetuate and reinforce the architecture of traditional accounting systems and thereby suffer many of the same weaknesses and criticisms. In a recent study, less than 15 percent of executives surveyed felt they were getting their money's worth from their IT investment.[4]

THE HEART OF THE PROBLEM

So why don't organizations get the same degree of help from their navigators and systems as found in today's F-15? The reasons are illustrated in Figure 1-1:

---

[3] R. Eccles, "The Performance Measurement Manifesto," *Harvard Business Review*, January-February 1991, p. 131.

[4] D.R. Vincent, "Information Technology—Should You Curtail Your Investment?," *Financial Executive*, May-June 1990, pp. 50-55.

FIGURE 1-1

The Heart of the Problem with Traditional Systems

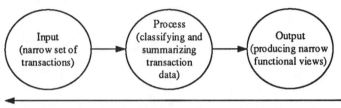

Narrow functional view drives the selection of transactions, the classifications, and summarization.

Each function or discipline within an organization uses IT to capture a limited set of transaction data, store a limited number of characteristics in a summarized format, and develop reports to meet the narrow objectives of a specific function. Therefore, each function (e.g. marketing, production, or accounting) has its own objectives and perspectives. For example, production focuses on building the product to be sold while many times ignoring marketing and accounting issues; marketing concentrates on selling something (which is sometimes as imaginary as real) ignoring the production and accounting ramifications; while accounting focuses only on accounting transactions and the financial impact of the transaction on the assets, liabilities, and owner's equity. Too often, organizationwide objectives and perspectives are not found outside the circles of organization executives.

The process of capturing, classifying, and summarizing transaction data is influenced by this narrow, functional view of the business. Therefore, each function develops its own way of processing business data to satisfy its own requirements. For example, production focuses on classifications for generating production schedules, marketing focuses on classifications for generating product margin and trend reports, while accountants focus on generating financial statements using the chart of accounts classification scheme. Once again, the organization as a whole is left without support for organizationwide planning, decision making, and objectives. Worse yet, the way data is processed tends to make the arbitrary boundaries between functions and disciplines even stronger.

The result of all this narrow-mindedness is that organizations are saddled with:

Inefficient and ineffective business processes

Unnecessary and burdensome organization structure

Inadequate measurements to guide management

Ineffective uses of information technology.

In short, when narrow functional views dominate the mind set of organization personnel, individuals and functions may well achieve their goals and objectives while the organization as a whole struggles. Likewise, individuals and functions may develop systems to support their narrow objectives, but the overall business objectives and perspectives are left largely unsupported.

THE CHALLENGE AND OPPORTUNITY

So, what can be done to address the problems we have discussed? Solving these problems requires changes in:

The nature of business processes

The way organizations are structured

The way business results are measured

The use of information technology.

Business solutions require much more than simply applying IT. Traditional IT applications that reflect the narrow functional mind-set have the characteristics illustrated in Figure 1–2. These systems are loosely connected by means of passing data from one to another resulting in tremendous duplication of effort and inefficient use of resources. We have found at least eight weaknesses common to all traditional systems built with a narrow functional mind-set (see Figure 1–3). The traditional accounting system probably illustrates the weaknesses more clearly than any other functional system. We will discuss the details and weaknesses of the traditional system's architecture in greater depth in Chapter Two.

Although IT is not a cure all, it can enable individuals and organizations to make tremendous changes toward the goal of developing business solutions. As Al Pipkin, controller for Coors Brewing Company, points out, IT is:

FIGURE 1-2
The Traditional Systems Architecture

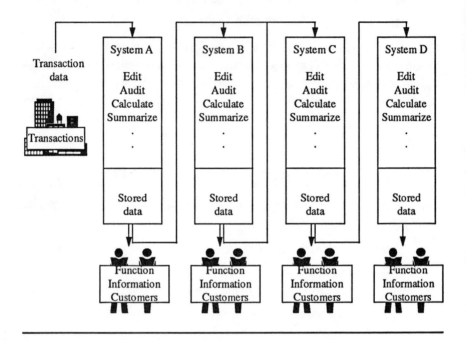

bringing about a total transformation of the controller's staff, and a re-definition of the overall financial system. Technology is changing the culture of the controller's organization just as it is impacting the entire business. In the 21st century, there will be fewer accountants on the controller's staff, but they will perform in totally new and exciting ways. You can pick up dozens of newspapers and magazines today that proclaim "the age of no paper is no longer a pipe dream." The drudgery of shuffling paper and doing routine manipulations of data soon will be gone. From now on, the controller's staff will add value to the business or it won't exist.[5]

Pipkin's observations apply to any business professional and the organization as a whole. In today's market, only organizations and individuals that provide value and an adequate return to investors and creditors survive. The

---

[5]A. Pipkin, "The 21st Century Controller," *Management Accounting*, February, 1989, p. 24.

FIGURE 1-3
Summary of Weaknesses

1. Stored data has limited characteristics about transactions.

2. Data classification schemes are not always appropriate or supportive.

3. Aggregation level of stored data is too high.

4. Useful integration of financial and nonfinancial data across the organization is difficult, if not impossible.

5. Recording, maintaining, and reporting processes seriously limit the system's ability to provide timely support for decision makers.

6. Traditional processing methods are not well adapted to changing business requirements.

7. Implementing and maintaining internal controls are costly, ineffective, and not performed in a timely manner.

8. Antiquated processing and storage methods are costly to maintain and operate.

market is becoming increasingly efficient at weeding out those who do not provide value, regardless of their stature and tenure in the market, or political power. Every day the media chronicle the demise of those who are unable to compete in this new business environment. Some manage to defer their demise through deceit, disguise, or political influence. Over time, however, only those which truly create value in a cost-effective manner remain viable.

The enabler for solving business problems, as Pipkin points out, is IT. So,

The challenge and the opportunity for contemporary organizations . . . is clear . . . systems can and should be designed to support the operations and the strategy of the organization. The technology exists to implement systems radically different from those being used today. What is lacking is knowledge.[6]

We now have the knowledge, as a result of research, collaboration, experimentation, and implementation, to develop business solutions radically different from the IT systems being developed and used today. Much of what has been learned is embodied in a set of solution concepts.

---

[6]H. T. Johnson and R. S. Kaplan, *Relevance Lost: The Rise and Fall of Management Accounting*, (Boston: Harvard Business School Press, 1987) p. 17-18.

SOLUTION CONCEPTS

In our own efforts, and our observations of successful efforts of others, we have identified five concepts that are critical to developing business solutions:

1. Focus on business events. The focus of attention must shift from narrow functional needs to the underlying business event. This shift in focus enables a horizontal (business process), instead of a vertical (functional), view of the business. Furthermore, focusing on business events enables organizations to simplify business processes, make changes in organization structures, change individual responsibilities, change measurement criteria, identify and control risk, and more effectively utilize information technology.

2. Simplify business processes and organizational structures. Before applying IT, the business process and the organization structure must be simplified. Once the critical essence of the process management structure is in place, IT can be applied to enable the new way of doing business.

3. Integrate data. Instead of dispersing and copying data throughout the organization, business event data must be integrated and made accessible to all information customers.

4. Integrate information processes and controls. Instead of being repeated throughout the organization, information processes and controls must be integrated and where possible, controls must be applied in real time.

5. Realign system component and business process ownership. The degree of success in implementing the prior solution concepts depends to a large extent on the degree to which changes are made in how information systems and business processes are owned and managed in organizations.

These solution concepts enable businesspeople to use technology to solve business problems. Application of the solution concepts results in a very different business and IT environment (see Figure 1–4). That environment is characterized by solutions that allow business data to be gathered and passed through a business event processor that executes relevant business and information process rules. The data are then stored in an integrated repository available to any authorized information customer. Organization structure can also be aligned with business processes rather than being bound to traditional

FIGURE 1-4
Enterprise Information Warehouse

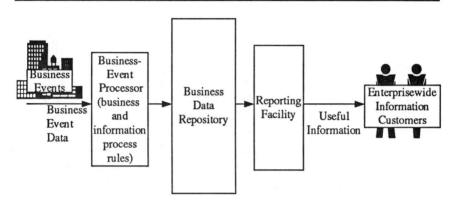

organization functions. Furthermore, the application of these solution concepts is not a one time effort which results in the optimal operation of an organization. Rather, it is the process of continual improvement which adapts to changing business requirements.

EVENT-DRIVEN BUSINESS SOLUTIONS

Although the concepts themselves are straightforward, applying them is no trivial task. However, the fact is, they do work. Let us mention just two examples as evidence.

Reimbursing Employees for Travel

IBM recently developed a solution for reimbursing over 200,000 domestic employees for travel expenses using the five solution concepts. The traditional reimbursement process is illustrated in Figure 1–5. The traditional business process and systems had many weaknesses. Utilizing the five solution concepts, IBM created an event-driven business solution called NEDS (National Employee Disbursement Solution). The architecture of the solution is illustrated in Figure 1–6.

FIGURE 1-5

Traditional Employee Reimbursement Process

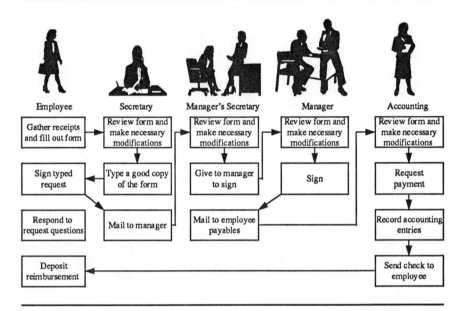

Employee	Secretary	Manager's Secretary	Manager	Accounting
Gather receipts and fill out form	Review form and make necessary modifications	Review form and make necessary modifications	Review form and make necessary modifications	Review form and make necessary modifications
Sign typed request	Type a good copy of the form	Give to manager to sign	Sign	Request payment
Respond to request questions	Mail to manager	Mail to employee payables		Record accounting entries
Deposit reimbursement				Send check to employee

The use of NEDS has resulted in IBM reassigning 80 percent of the employees assigned to build, maintain, and use prior reimbursement systems. The 17 systems supporting the traditional reimbursement process have been replaced by the one business solution—NEDS. Overall, NEDS and related changes will save IBM over $300 million during the next 10 years. This savings reflects nothing of the increased power for management equipped with more useful information to negotiate contracts with travel and lodging providers and to monitor the value and effectiveness of travel.

Not only is NEDS being used to reimburse employees for travel expenses, it is now being expanded to serve as the platform for processing all employee claims against IBM (e.g., wages, reimbursements, benefits, and loans). One solution will handle what has traditionally required several systems. Furthermore, this solution is enabling significant changes in the management structure of the reimbursement process and in the roles and responsibilities of those supporting process management.

These solution concepts have not only been applied in corporate settings, they have been applied in nonprofit settings as well.

FIGURE 1-6
NEDS Architecture

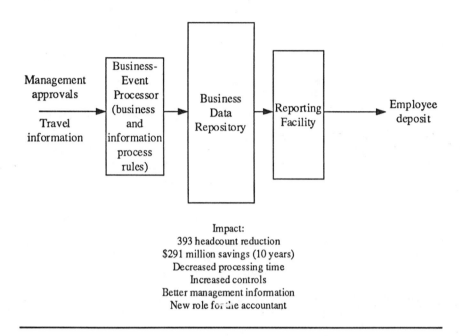

Impact:
393 headcount reduction
$291 million savings (10 years)
Decreased processing time
Increased controls
Better management information
New role for the accountant

Oregon Department of Transportation

In 1989 state auditors declared Oregon's Department of Transportation (DOT) accounting system unauditable. The system was unable to account for millions of dollars of state funds. A new controller was hired to resolve the problems. With the help of Rick Roth and others from Price Waterhouse's Office of Government Services, the five solution concepts we have discussed were applied. Within months the financial processes were under control, needed financial information was being provided, and the accounting staff was cut from over 125 people to fewer than 50.

The role of the remaining accountants has changed substantially. Accountants are now viewed as business solution professionals who are responsible for helping identify, implement, and maintain business rules and who support management decision making by analyzing business data and providing useful information to decision makers. They no longer spend their time performing primarily clerical tasks to maintain only limited financial data. Instead, these business solution professionals are directed to meet with DOT management and engineers to see what problems they can help solve. Furthermore, state auditors have concluded that the new event-driven business solution is extremely well controlled and easy to audit. Audits now are performed in a fraction of the time required in the past and are much more thorough.

Other examples could be cited, but suffice it to say, the concepts work. They result in very different business and information processes and create an environment in which these processes can evolve to meet the changing needs of the business.

We are proposing a next step in the evolution of business problem solving using IT (Figure 1–7). The key to success is financial and information professionals working together to create what we call a business solution professional. Together, the CFO and CIO have access to nearly all business processes, they have the organizational muscle to facilitate and encourage change, and they have access to executives. Apart, their capabilities are limited and their usefulness, over the long term, is marginal. To create the business solutions organizations need today, the two must work together. You

FIGURE 1-7
Evolution of Business Systems

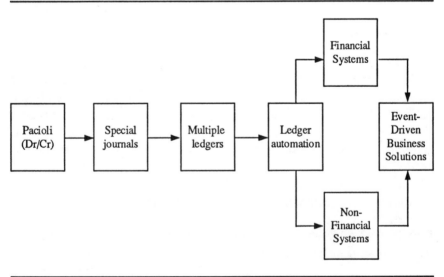

can now see why we described the new business solution professional playing a very different role. Certainly, this will require significant change.

THE CALL FOR CHANGE

Overcoming weaknesses in functionally oriented systems, adopting new information concepts, and creating business solution professionals require change: change that threatens some and leads them to "circle the wagons" to fend off the attacking heathens. We believe all this represents tremendous opportunities. Accounting and IT professionals have a strategic opportunity, as at no other time in their professional histories, to contribute greater value to their organizations and to society by being the catalyst for moving the organization into the future. The trick is knowing where to head. Wayne Gretzki offers some timely, and worthwhile, advice. When asked why he is so successful in hockey, he responded, "I skate where I think the puck will be, not where it is." In this book, we describe where the puck is headed. That is, we describe the future use of IT by organizations and the role of accounting and IT professionals.

The likelihood of successfully developing business solutions is increased substantially by combining the efforts of accounting and IT professionals. We fully recognize the danger in suggesting that these two professions merge their skills and responsibilities. Accounting and IT professionals have had a somewhat love/hate relationship over the past 30 years. The verbal barbs of "bean counter" and "bit head" are freely thrown back and forth. Using the metaphor of a romance, each organization can find the relationship between their accounting and IT professionals at some point along a time line with three general phases: the first kiss, the separation, and the courtship and marriage. Although there are exceptions, we have found the metaphor all too descriptive of most organizations.

The First Kiss

Many first-time applications of information technology in business are for accounting tasks that manually may take several people countless hours and reams of paper. These tasks can suddenly be performed by a single computer in a fraction of the time and with far fewer mistakes. Nearly any organization can quickly automate many of the clerical processes involved in payroll, accounts receivable, accounts payable, and general ledger functions. The increased efficiency and accuracy of using advanced information technology is typically welcomed enthusiastically by both accountants and management alike. With the application of IT, it appears accounting systems finally reach their maturity. Since the vast majority of initial computer applications are for accounting tasks, the accounting function maintains control over the application of IT in these organizations.

The Separation

Soon after the application of IT to accounting processes, the wisdom of accountants managing IT resources comes into question as management begins to ask for IT applications outside the traditional scope of accounting. For example, why can't IT be used to monitor production processes, provide demographic information about customers, help monitor the productivity of key production personnel, or help solve a myriad of other business problems facing management? Each of these requests focus on improving the support for decision making, improving business and information processes, or improving controls over risk. However, these requests go beyond the traditional accounting responsibilities of summarizing the financial impact of the organization's business processes.

Intentionally or otherwise, accounting professionals begin to distance themselves from the new demands of management because "that's not accounting." The question is not whether it is accounting; the issue is that the accountant quickly realizes the limitations of the traditional accounting system architecture in meeting the broader information needs of management. As a result, the IT professional emerges.[7] What is interesting is that from the very outset, IT professionals view their mission as supporting the requirements of all information customers. If you think about this carefully, IT professionals include accounting information within their scope of purpose. From the IT perspective, accounting spins off a discipline (IT) bigger than itself, which can legitimately be viewed to include traditional accounting.

---

[7]Other common names for this specialization include Information Systems, Management Information Systems, Decision Support, or Business Systems. We are not including in this designation the more engineering-related professionals commonly known as computer scientists. These individuals focus on developing IT itself while IT professionals concentrate on applying IT.

The rift between IT and accounting generally deepens in practice and theory. Each becomes very leery of the other. The result is a poorly coordinated, organizationwide use of information technology to support the business. Not only can a rift develop between IT and accounting, IT often becomes a battleground among the various functional areas of an organization. Organizations may invest large amounts of money to install and maintain a new suite of IT applications that are redundant at best, and downright counterproductive at worst.

As the situation worsens, IT professionals often find themselves lacking the enterprisewide muscle they once enjoyed with accounting to effect necessary changes and are unable to direct critical organizationwide changes in the use of IT. In such situations, the best an organization can hope for is two competing architectures—the accounting system architecture and the nonfinancial systems architecture—neither of which provides a solution to the overall problem of effectively using IT to solve business problems. Most organizations typically end up with several competing architectures across the wide variety of nonfinancial systems.

Not only is there tremendous waste in developing and operating these systems, executive level management often receives conflicting data from the various information subsystems. The resulting value and reliability of IT applications begin to be questioned. Some may even begin to seriously talk about the "good old days before computers." Equally aggravating, however, is the fact that executives see these systems as using significant amounts of their resources to generate enormous amounts of data, but yielding very little return on their investment. At this stage organizations often consider themselves data-rich but information-poor. Although this period might be labeled the "dark days" of the accounting/IT relationship, relatively new information concepts and technologies offer hope for a brighter future.

The Courtship and Marriage

Eventually management, accounting, and IT professionals recognize the tremendous waste of resources in their separate activities. Working together, they begin experimenting with various information concepts and technologies to develop new and exciting solutions that use IT to better support decision makers, while also making the business and information processes more efficient, effective, and better controlled. These solutions save organization resources and significantly increase the value of both accounting and IT professionals.

As the successful marriage of accounting and IT becomes known, management of other organizations is arranging some shotgun marriages. Some accounting and IT professionals see the writing on the wall. A few resist with a religious-like fervor that would make Joan of Arc proud. However, the direction is clear—the skill sets of accounting and IT professionals can, must, and are merging to create a new information professional. As we have already mentioned, the key to success for the new information professional is to view each new challenge to their role or system as an opportunity rather than a threat.

Peter Drucker sums up the accounting/IT relationship noting that in many organizations the two still:

> have different backgrounds, different values, different career ladders. They work in different departments and for different bosses. There is a "chief information officer" for computer-based data processing, usually with a background in computer technology. Accounting typically reports to a "chief financial officer," often with a background in financing the company and in managing its money. Neither boss, in other words, is information-focused as a rule.[8]

We need a new professional that can help develop solutions for the business, not just accounting or technological, problems.

NEW SKILLS FOR THE NEW WORLD

The new business solution professional serves much the same role as the pilot's navigator. To a large extent, business solution professionals combine many of the traditional skills of both accounting and IT, along with other skills not currently found in either. Accountants typically have a good business foundation and experience with controlling risk, but have a hard time taking advantage of the capabilities provided by current information concepts and technologies. IT professionals understand current information concepts and technology but typically lack good business sense or in-depth understanding

---

[8]P. Drucker, "Be Data Literate—Know What to Know," *The Wall Street Journal*, December 1, 1992, p. C1.

of business processes and objectives, being more enamored with technological glitz than solving business problems. Furthermore, as Peter Drucker notes, neither typically understands the requirements to support the decision making required of today's information customers.

Encouraging and facilitating the creation of business solution professionals requires leadership. This leadership cannot come from traditional-minded management who think and act in traditional ways. Tom Peters in his book *Liberation Management* makes this point abundantly clear. New business solution professionals require new leaders with an amalgam of skills not commonly found in functionally oriented, tradition-bound managers.

Let us suggest a few of the more essential skills new business solution professionals must possess.

Understand the Nature of Business Processes

The Index Group, a well-known management consulting group, recently surveyed several IT executives regarding key issues for future IT professionals. At the top of the list was the need to understand business processes.[9] They found that technically elegant IT applications were frequently developed which did little to really help the business.

Our experience with accounting professionals suggests a similar need. The accounting process is so detached from the ongoing operations of the business that many times the accountant can work largely ignorant of the nature of business processes and the issues facing management. Therefore, both accounting and IT professionals must become students of business processes and focus on developing solutions for business processes.

Aggressively Support Decision Making

Decision support can be provided in three ways:

Provide useful information

Provide methods for improving decision making

Automate decisions when appropriate, justified, and possible.

---

[9]D. Eskow, "IS Chiefs Seek to Revamp Business Processes," *PC Week*, February 12, 1990, p. 12.

Traditionally, IT has been used primarily to provide useful information. However, as we noted above, there are two other significant means of improving decision making. We will concentrate only on providing useful information in this book. However, the concepts we introduce in this book can greatly increase the feasibility of the other two methods of supporting decision making.

Useful information is a term that is little understood and often overused. For information to be useful it must be both relevant and reliable. It includes a description of what has happened while providing a basis for predicting the future. Rather than entering into an endless debate over exactly what is useful information about a business to support decision making, we believe one simple rule resolves the question:

The information customer is the final arbiter of any debate over what is useful information.

Unless information is provided in a timely manner, its value to information customers diminishes significantly. Decision making regarding organizations is ongoing. Many times decision makers do not have the luxury of saying, "Oh, I don't have the information needed to make that decision so I will just wait to make any decisions." Although deferring the decision may be appropriate at times, it certainly could not be followed regularly without seriously affecting the organization's performance and ability to continue creating value. Therefore, unless timely information is provided to decision makers, the decision maker is left to either defer the decision or project the outcome.

For the new business solution professional, the information customer (e.g. management, investor, regulator, or lawmaker), not the provider (accountant or otherwise), is the final arbiter of what is useful information. Our experience indicates that information customers have a broad range of information requirements that extend far beyond the traditional accounting domain. The individuality of decision processes and the diversity of decisions involved in planning, controlling, and evaluating an organization demand access to an equally diverse set of information.

Accountants particularly, must relinquish the notion "I only do numbers" and stop the endless debate over what is, and is not, accounting. The debate should focus on what is useful, deferring to the information customer when at an impasse.

View Change as an Opportunity Instead of a Threat

Today's economic environment underscores the need for continual change in business and information processes. The steady and somewhat predictable business environment of the past has been replaced by a truly dynamic economy. We should not be surprised then by the need for accounting and IT professionals to change. Change should be viewed as both essential and as fortuitous. Unfortunately, most people do not see accountants as facilitators of change.

The attitude needed by accounting and IT professionals was illustrated in a movie several years ago about a submarine and its crew during World War II. In the movie, Tony Curtis played the part of a military entrepreneur. At one point in the film enemy airplanes began attacking the submarine while it was docked. Rather than running for cover, Curtis ran for the nearest truck and began to drive off. The commanding officer of the sub asked what he was doing. Curtis responded, "Confusion is opportunity" and drove off to cash in on the current opportunity.

Now, we are not suggesting that we need a bevy of black market shysters who take advantage of anyone and everyone. What we do need, however, are professionals who are not threatened by the need for change and who respond to change with timeliness and creativity.

Balancing Change and Controlling Risk

A critical aspect of seizing opportunities is balancing the need for making business processes as effective and efficient as possible while controlling business and information processing risks. All too often, these two objectives are viewed as competing, if not mutually exclusive. However, this need not be the case.

We do not advocate, or believe in, the thought that business processes can become perfectly efficient and effective, or that risks can be perfectly controlled. We do believe, however, that we can do much better than we are currently doing in both areas. We must strike an appropriate balance between the two. This is both desirable and achievable.

Focus on Business Solutions, Not IT Applications

For some accountants, having to understand the nature of IT, let alone its business value, results in an overwhelming challenge. Some accountants pride themselves on having avoided the use of technology for so long. Such "achievements" can no longer be tolerated if we are to balance continual improvement through the use of information technology and the need for controlling risk. IT must be viewed as a powerful tool to help solve business problems, not as a threat that opens a business to uncontrollable risk.

For IT professionals, focusing on the business value of IT is outside the scope of what they feel is their strength. Too often we are wowed by engineering specifications, instead of the business value, of new technologies. Too many times, the heart of a proposal for new technology is more for glitz than for business value. What we need are professionals with sound business judgment who are able to utilize IT to solve business problems, not just apply IT to traditional business and information processes. Business solutions facilitate continual improvement in business and information processes, organization structures, use of IT, and business measurements.

Become Involved in the Solution Development Process

IT professionals have traditionally taken the lead in applying information technology, with accountants playing only a tangential role. Systems development processes which preclude everyone but those skilled in the elaborate methodologies have prevented more widespread involvement. We see the need to have both accounting and IT skills equally involved in the development of business solutions. A large part of this book focuses on simplifying the development process and identifying the objectives, techniques, and tools necessary for the IT neophyte to play a critical role in, or even lead, the solution development process. Our position was supported recently when DMR, a leading provider of information technology services called for businesspeople, not IT professionals, to take the lead in developing business solutions utilizing IT.[10]

---

[10]"Open Systems: Managing the Transition, Part II," Special Edition of *Business Week*: *Reinventing America*, 1992.

CARPE DIEM (SEIZE THE DAY)!

The skills and services of the business solution professional, which we expect to continue expanding in the future, can be of tremendous value to organizations. Furthermore, we fully expect the list of essential skills to continue to grow. The key is for the business solution professional to be value-driven, not regulation-, technology-, or tradition-driven. Certainly, we must not violate regulations or ignore tradition and technological capabilities. By the same token, we should not confuse tradition with regulation.

This is a strategic opportunity for those willing to change. We are not, however, attempting to trivialize the difficulty of changing professions, perceptions, or processes. Machiavelli was insightful when he observed:

It must be considered that there is nothing more difficult to carry out, nor more doubtful of success, nor more dangerous to handle than to initiate a new order of things. For the reformer has enemies in all those who profit by the old order, and only lukewarm defenders by all those who could profit by the new order. This lukewarmness arises partly from fear of their adversaries who have the laws in their favor, and partly from the incredulity of mankind who do not truly believe in anything new until they have had actual experience with it.[11]

We are convinced that people and organizations can and must change. As Tom Peters points out:

The way we organize to get things done in the public and private sectors, and in general, is undergoing the most profound shift since (at least) the Industrial Revolution. It's no wonder that we all—clerk, middle manager, government minister, and chairman of the board alike—feel a disquiet, bordering on despair, that goes far beyond the only somewhat gloomy economic statistics . . . The story that unfolds—from CNN to The Body Shop (and even the Union Pacific Railroad)—is in equal parts terrifying and liberating. Terrifying because all old bets are off, from the boardroom (which *may* disappear) to the factory (which, in the form we've lived with for the last 150 years, *will* disappear). Liberating because there's never been a time so laden with opportunity for anyone, receptionist or bank president, with a mind to shuck tradition and take the plunge.[12]

---

[11]N. Machiavelli, *The Prince*, Translated by Luigi Rice, Rev. E.R.P. Vincent, (New York: New American Library; 1952) p. 10.

[12]T. Peters, *Liberation Management: Necessary Disorganization for the Nanosecond Nineties*, (New York: Alfred A. Knopf, 1992), p. 345.

Once someone decides to take the plunge, some guidance as to the direction of the plunge helps make the difference between a bellyflop and a swan dive. This book focuses on providing the necessary direction for those who are motivated to take the plunge to apply the solution concepts to create useful business solutions.

Chapter Two

An Accounting Example
Why It Is Broken and Concepts to Fix It.

IT'S BROKE!

Chapter One summarized the weaknesses of traditional systems that focus on a narrow set of business events, summarize and classify the data, and report by functional areas. These systems are built to accomplish a single, narrow focus rather than address organizationwide needs. Probably the best example is the traditional accounting system.

Today many people are complaining that traditional accounting suffers from many weaknesses and is not addressing the needs of information customers both within and without organizations. For example, Bob Elliott, partner in the national office of KPMG/Peat Marwick recently said, "Our U.S. accounting paradigm is important to our national competitiveness, is 'broke,' and needs fixing."[1] Elliott is not alone in his criticisms. In a scathing opinion of corruption-run-amok at Charles Keating, Jr.'s Lincoln Savings & Loan trial, U.S. District Court Judge Stanley Sporkin concluded that the "system of accounting that exists in the United States is in a sorry state."[2]

Several others are equally critical.[3] Before attempting to fix the problems, we need to understand a little more about the nature of the accounting system.

---

[1]R.K. Elliott, "U.S. Accounting: A National Emergency," *Financial Reporting and Standard Setting* (New York: American Institute of Certified Public Accountants, 1991), p. 13.

[2]R. Wyden, "The First Line of Defense," *New Accountant*, December 1990, pp. 14–16.

[3]Some examples of those critical of the traditional accounting system include:

H.T. Johnson and R. S. Kaplan, *Relevance Lost: The Rise and Fall of Management Accounting*, (Boston: Harvard Business School Press, 1987).

D. A. Curtis, *Management Rediscovered: How Companies Can Escape the Numbers Trap* (Homewood, Ill. Richard D. Irwin, 1990).

W. E. McCarthy, "The REA Accounting Model: A Generalized Framework for Accounting Systems in a Shared Data Environment," *The Accounting Review*, July 1982, pp. 554–77.

We will then generalize these observations to include business systems in general. This chapter is not intended to provide an exhaustive tutorial regarding the establishment or operation of a traditional accounting process. Our interest is in evaluating the fundamental characteristics of the process to identify ways in which it can be improved, thereby increasing its value to the organization. Our purpose is to establish a foundation upon which we can critically evaluate the traditional accounting process and its value to the business. Let us begin by looking at the conceptual foundations for the traditional accounting system.

PACIOLI: THE FATHER OF TRADITIONAL ACCOUNTING

The birth of the traditional accounting process is typically credited to a Franciscan monk named Luca Pacioli (pronounced Pa-chol-ee) who lived in Italy during the 1500s. Although the initial ideas proposed by Pacioli have been modified over the years, the essence of his original proposal remains intact.

At the heart of Pacioli's concept is the chart of accounts. The chart of accounts is used to classify financial measurements of an organization's assets, liabilities, and equity. Data organized using a chart of accounts classification scheme is typically summarized using at least two financial statements. Data describing financial results of operations for a specific time period are summarized in an Income Statement, while data describing the financial position of the organization at a point in time are summarized in a Balance Sheet. Accounts summarized on the Income Statement are called *nominal* accounts, while accounts summarized on the Balance Sheet are called *real* accounts.

A sample chart of accounts and financial statements are shown in Figures 2–1, 2–2, and 2–3. Because each industry and organization is different, so is each organization's chart of accounts. One of the more useful compendiums of the various types of charts of accounts and processing descriptions is *The Encyclopedia of Accounting Systems,*[4] which summarizes the nature of

---

[4]*The Encyclopedia of Accounting Systems,* 2nd edition (Englewood Cliffs, NJ: Prentice Hall, 1974).

FIGURE 2-1
Sample Chart of Accounts

Accounting Title	Account Number
Current Assets:	
Cash	110
Accounts Receivable	130
Research Fees Receivable	140
Supplies Inventory	160
Prepaid Insurance	180
Property, Plant, and Equipment	
Land	210
Building	220
Accumulated Depreciation	
- Building	230
Equipment	240
Accumulated Depreciation	
- Equipment	250
Current Liabilities:	
Accounts Payable	310
Income Taxes Payable	330
Salaries Payable	340
Interest Payable	350
Cash Dividends Payable	360
Services to Be Rendered	380

Accounting Title	Account Number
Long-Term Debt:	
Notes Payable	410
Stockholder's Equity:	
Capital Stock	510
Retained Earnings	550
Revenue and Expense Summary	590
Revenue:	
Revenue from Services	610
Expenses:	
Salaries Expense	710
Supplies Expense	720
Depreciation Expense - Equipment	730
Depreciation Expense - Building	810
Insurance Expense	820
Other Administrative Expenses	890
Interest Expense	910
Federal Income Taxes	950

Adapted from: J.L. Boockholdt, *Accounting Information Systems: Transaction Processing and Controls,* 3rd ed. (Homewood, Ill.: Richard D. Irwin, 1993).

traditional accounting systems for industries ranging from agriculture to zoos.

To record accounting data using the chart of accounts classification scheme, Pacioli proposed the double entry accounting system. Charles Sprague, an accounting scholar who codified much of contemporary accounting theory in the early 1900s, explained the nature of this process:

Any occurrence [accounting transaction] must be either an increase or a decrease of values, and there are three classes of values [assets, liabilities, and equity]; hence there are six possible occurrences:

1. Increase of Assets.
2. Decrease of Assets.
3. Increase of Liability.
4. Decrease of Liability.

FIGURE 2-2
Sample Income Statement

ALPHA RESEARCH CORPORATION
Income Statement
for Month Ended September 30, 19XX

Revenue from Services		$12,200
Expenses:		
Salaries Expense	$6,600	
Supplies Expense	900	
Depreciation Expense - Equipment	1,200	
Depreciation Expense - Building	500	
Insurance Expense	25	
Interest Expense	_314_	
Total Expenses		_9,539_
Net Income Before Taxes		$ 2,661
Income Taxes		_700_
Net Income		1,961

Adapted from: J.L. Boockholdt, *Accounting Information Systems: Transaction Processing and Controls*, 3rd ed. (Homewood, Ill.: Richard D. Irwin, 1993).

---

5. Increase of Proprietorship [equity].
6. Decrease of Proprietorship [equity].

Balances of assets belong on the debit (left) side; therefore, increases are debits and decreases are credits. Balances of liabilities are credits; therefore increases of liabilities are credits and decreases are debits. Balances of proprietorship are credits; therefore increases of proprietorship are credits and decreases are debits. We have therefore the six possible occurrences distributed as follows under debits and credits:

FIGURE 2-3
Sample Balance Sheet

ALPHA RESEARCH CORPORATION			Liabilitites and Stockholdeers' Equity	
Balance Sheet				
As of September 30, 19XX				
Assets				
			Current Liabilities:	
Current Assets:			Notes Payable (current portion)	$10,000
Cash		$62,000	Salaries Payable	600
Accounts Receivable		1,200	Interest Payable	314
Research Fees Receivable		4,000	Services to Be Rendered	55,000
Supplies Inventory		5,100	Total Current Liabilities	65,914
Prepaid Insurance		275		
Total Current Assets		72,575	Long-Term Debt:	
Property, Plant, and Equipment:			Notes Payable (long-term portion)	55,000
Land	$20,000			
Building	$60,000		Stockholders' Equity:	
Acc Depreciation 500	59,500		Capital Stock, par $100,	
Equipment 72,000			(1,000 shares outstanding) $100,000	
Acc Depreciation 1,200	70,800	150,300	Retained Earnings 1,961	101,961
Total Assets		$222,875	Total Liabilities and Stockholders' Equity	$222,875

Adapted from: J.L. Boockholdt, *Accounting Information Systems: Transaction Processing and Controls*, 3rd ed. (Homewood, Ill.: Richard D. Irwin, 1993).

Debits
(Entries on the left side)
Increase of Assets
Decrease of Liabilities
Decrease of Proprietorship (Equity)

Credits
(Entries on the right side)
Decrease of Assets
Increase of Liabilities
Increase of Proprietorship (Equity)

. . . in every transaction at least two of the occurrences must appear . . . on opposite sides of the above list.[5]

When the accounts are in balance the following equation is maintained:

Assets = Liabilities + Equity

There is really nothing magic about the preceding equation. It is simply one of many models of an organization's economics. In and of itself, it does not

[5]C. Sprague, *The Philosophy of Accounts* (Lawrence, Kansas: Scholars Book Co., 1907, 1908, 1972), pp. 23–24.

keep the company economically viable or "balanced." Rather, it formalizes one financially oriented view of the organization's activities and resources. Furthermore, it is not intended to be the best, or only, financial view of the organization.

Once the double entry approach is adopted, whatever the economic reality being represented, the accounts must be kept in balance. To keep the accounts in balance, Pacioli proposed a fairly rigid process for recording, maintaining, and reporting accounting transaction data. Again, the process, like the underlying concepts, has been modified at times, but the underlying nature of the process remains essentially the same as when Pacioli first introduced it.

THE TRADITIONAL ACCOUNTING PROCESS

Inherent in the traditional process of recording, maintaining, and reporting accounting data is a variety of mechanisms for reducing human error and keeping an organization's transaction data in balance. Each step of the process is performed in a specific order. The end result of the process is the creation of an organization's financial statements (e.g., balance sheet, income statement, and statement of changes in financial position) with a minimal amount of error. Let's look at the nature of each step in the process using the illustration in Figure 2–4.

Select and Analyze Transaction Data

The accounting process actually begins outside the accounting domain. The person representing the organization who is participating in the event prepares documentation about its occurrence. Over time, if not during the design of the system, the accountant identifies which types of event documentation are needed as input to the accounting system by asking two important questions:

1. Does the event affect the financial statements of the organization?
2. Can the effect of the event be measured financially?

If the answer to the first question is no, the accountant essentially ignores the occurrence of the event. The event data may be recorded in one or more

FIGURE 2-4
The Traditional Accounting Process

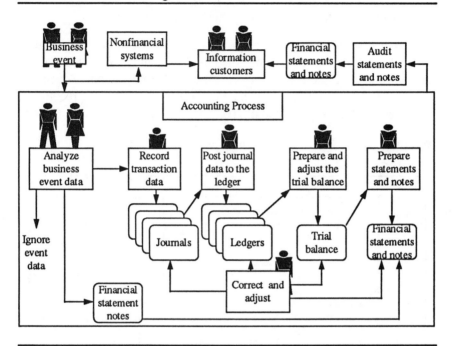

of the nonfinancial systems outside the accounting process. If the answer is yes, then the accountant calls the business event an accounting transaction and then asks the second question. For transactions that cannot be reliably measured in financial terms, the accountant flags the transaction for later use while preparing the financial statement notes. Transactions for which the financial effect is measurable result in the accountant recording the data in the accounting journals.

An important point to make here is that, from the onset, financial and nonfinancial data are largely separated. This makes it very difficult, if not impossible, to integrate the two later at any meaningful level of detail.

Record Transaction Data

Recording accounting transaction data involves two steps:

1. Interpret the effect of the accounting transaction on the organization's financial statements.
2. Record the transaction data in the accounting journals.

Having identified an accounting transaction, the accountant begins filtering and summarizing the data captured by determining which accounts are affected and by selecting and/or calculating the data on the source document to record (e.g., date and financial amount). The complete entry is recorded in a journal, such as the general journal (see Figure 2–5). Sometimes additional

FIGURE 2-5

Sample General Journal

Date		Accounts and Explanations	Ref	Debit	Credit
Sep	1	Cash		100,000	
		Capital Stock			100,000
		Issued capital stock for cash.			
	2	Land		20,000	
		Building		60,000	
		Cash			15,000
		Notes Payable			65,000
		Purchased land and building financed in part by a long-term note.			
	3	Equipment		72,000	
		Cash			72,000
		Cash purchase of equipment.			
	4	Supplies Inventory		6,000	
		Accounts Payable			6,000
		Supplies purchased from General Chemical Corporation on account.			
	5	Cash		60,000	
		Services to Be Rendered			60,000
		Advanced payment by Delta Aircraft Company for contract signed.			

Adapted from: J.L. Boockholdt, *Accounting Information Systems: Transaction Processing and Controls*, 3rd ed. (Homewood, Ill.: Richard D. Irwin, 1993).

explanatory notes may accompany the date, account, and amount data as well. Regardless, the accountant is responsible to make sure all entries are properly recorded so as to keep the accounting equation (Assets = Liabilities + Equity) in balance.

Understanding the rules by which source document data are translated into accounting journal entries and handling the large variety and volume of transactions is no small task. Many organizations have accounting personnel and systems dedicated to subsets of transactions such as accounts receivable (sales and cash receipts) or accounts payable (purchases and cash disbursements). Some organizations are so large they must assign accounting personnel responsibility for only a small portion of a specific part of the accounting records (e.g., accounts receivable for customers located in New York, checks issued for payroll, or purchases from one specific vendor).

Once accounting transactions are properly interpreted and recorded, much of the remaining accounting process is clerical in nature. The next step is to post the journal entries to the ledger.

Post Journal Data to Ledgers

The ledger is essentially a columnar pad as shown in Figure 2–6. One column of the ledger is used for debit entries, one column for credit entries, and one column for the ledger account balance. Reference data are also included to link ledger entries to the journals. Each ledger account serves as an information bucket. Posting to the ledger continues the summarization of raw accounting data begun while recording journal entries. The posting process is quite simple. At the end of a specified period of time, which can range from the end of each day to the end of each month, the data on each line of each general journal entry is copied into the appropriate ledger summarizing data for that particular account.

When special journals are used the posting process is more efficient. Special purpose journals are used to summarize accounting transactions that are all of the same type such as sales, cash receipts, and cash disbursements. These journals make the posting process much more efficient by reducing the need to copy the details of each transaction from the general journal to the ledgers. Instead, only the total of the journal for the day, week, or month is posted and the detail remains in the special journal.

Many accounting systems today attempt to support multiple financial reporting requirements for financial, tax, and managerial use by having

FIGURE 2-6

Sample Ledger Layout

Account Title	Cash		Account Number		110	
Date	Description	Ref	Debit	Credit	Balance
Sep 1		1	100,000		100,000
2		1		15,000	85,000
3		1		72,000	13,000
5		1	60,000		73,000

multiple sets of ledgers. In some countries the structure of the chart of accounts is prescribed by law. In such cases, a consolidated ledger is maintained along with ledgers for each particular reporting or statutory requirement.

Organizations with a variety of subsidiary operations located in different countries, each with their own chart of accounts, require hundreds if not thousands of accounts and accountants to keep all the different systems in sync. What seems so simple initially quickly becomes quite complex, particularly when the reporting requirements become more and more diverse.

Whether using a single journal and chart of accounts, or multiple journals and charts of accounts, eventually the ledgers are used to prepare a trial balance for the organization.

Prepare and Adjust the Trial Balance

The trial balance is a listing of the organization's chart of accounts along with each account balance (see Figure 2–7). If the transaction data have been

FIGURE 2-7

Sample Trial Balance

	Debit	Credit
110 Cash	$ 62,000	
130 Accounts Receivable	1,200	
140 Research Fees Receivable	4,000	
160 Supplies Inventory	5,100	
180 Prepaid Insurance	275	
210 Land	20,000	
220 Building	60,000	
230 Accumulated Depreciation - Building		500
240 Equipment	72,000	
250 Accumulated Depreciation - Equipment		1,200
340 Salaries Payable		600
350 Interest Payable		314
380 Services to Be Rendered		55,000
410 Notes Payable		65,000
510 Capital Stock		100,000
610 Revenue from Services		12,200
710 Salaries Expense	6,600	
720 Supplies Expense	900	
730 Depreciation Expense - Equipment	1,200	
810 Depreciation Expense - Building	500	
820 Insurance Expense	25	
910 Interest Expense	314	
950 Federal Income Tax	700	
	$234,814	$234,814

Adapted from: J.L. Boockholdt, *Accounting Information Systems: Transaction Processing and Controls*, 3rd ed. (Homewood, Ill.: Richard D. Irwin, 1993).

---

properly recorded and posted, the total debits and credits of the trial balance should be equal. If they are not, then the accountant must identify the errors in the accounting process, sometimes going back to the transaction documentation. This can be a maddening experience for even a small set of books. Once the trail balance is in balance, the accountant is ready to make any reporting period adjustments to the account balances before preparing the financial statements.

It is important to note that having a trial balance in balance simply assures the debits and credits recorded in the system are equal. The trial balance does not ensure transaction data is either complete or accurate. The task of testing the completeness and accuracy of the data is left to the auditor.

Adjusting entries are recorded to recognize a variety of changes in the financial condition of the organization's assets and liabilities ranging from asset utilization to the accrual of various liabilities. These entries are actually made through the general journal and posted to the ledger accounts. Once all the adjustments have been recorded, they are posted to the ledger accounts and then summarized in an adjusted trial balance.

Prepare Financial Statements and Notes

With the trial balance complete, the financial statements are generated by selecting the accounts that appear on each statement. Typically, the financial statements aggregate the detailed trial balance account data into much more highly summarized categories. The primary reason for not including the entire trial balance is more for pragmatic reasons. Some charts of accounts for large organizations can involve literally hundreds if not thousands of accounts. Therefore, the information is summarized yet again for the user.

Explanatory notes are included with the statements to provide additional information that may be useful to the financial statement user. This may include information about accounting transaction data which is somewhat subjective but important when attempting to assess the financial well-being of the organization. This may include notes about impending law suits, the impact of natural disasters, the effect of political strife, or a variety of other issues which have an impact on the financial health of the organization.

A closing process is used to reduce the balance in the nominal accounts to zero and reflect the results of operations for the period in owner's equity. This step is typically referred to as closing the ledger. The reason for using the word closing is that in a manual system the physical books containing the nominal ledger account data are closed and new physical books are opened to record the next period's nominal accounting data.

Audit Financial Statements

Publicly owned enterprises whose stock is traded on a public exchange are required to publish their financial statements. Before the statements can be released they must be audited by someone certified to do so. Other organizations not required by statute to release their financial statements may still have audits in accordance with owners' directives, creditor's requirements, or as a matter of caution. In the United States, individuals are required to be Certified Public Accountants (CPAs) to audit financial statements for public disclosure.

The purpose of the audit is to determine whether the statements fairly present the financial performance and position of the organization in accordance with generally accepted accounting principles. Auditing involves assessing the organization's business and information processing controls, sampling detailed data supporting each account, investigating the existence of key assets, assessing whether the records are complete, and a variety of similar activities. Most of this work is performed at the close of a reporting period. Assuming the auditor does not find any evidence of wrongdoing or improper record-keeping, the financial statements are given a "clean opinion" and the statements are prepared for distribution.

The formality of distributing financial statements ranges from simply mailing them to investors and creditors to holding precisely coordinated news conferences in key financial markets throughout the world. Regardless of the formality, the financial statements and notes are made available to financial statement users.

As you can see, the accounting process is anything but trivial. To the extent the financial statements are useful, the accounting process is a valuable part of helping an organization run effectively. Our purpose in reviewing the nature of the accounting process is to level set everyone in preparation for a critical look at the traditional accounting system.

WEAKNESSES OF THE ACCOUNTING SYSTEM

Although the traditional accounting system has its strengths, several individuals, groups, and organizations are becoming increasingly critical of it. The question we must answer is, "Why?" Are there good reasons for their criticisms? If there are valid criticisms, can we identify the problems and correct them?

Criticisms of traditional accounting systems center around eight significant weakness. These criticisms are from an enterprise perspective, looking at the enterprise as a whole, not simply the accountant's view. An enterprise perspective looks at the solution requirements across the entire organization including marketing, production, finance, logistics, executives, and others. Specifically, we want to see how well the accounting system facilitates continual improvement in business and information processes, organization structures, use of IT, and business measurements. An enterprise perspective is important because businesspeople, not accountants, are the customers.

Of these eight weaknesses, *four deal with data and four deal with process* (see Figure 2–8). The first four weaknesses deal with the nature and organization of data within the system and were first proposed by Bill McCarthy.[6] We have made some modifications, but the basic ideas are his. The last four weaknesses deal with the way accounting data are processed and are dependent, to some degree, on the data related weaknesses. Once the data-related weaknesses are addressed, the processing-related issues are much easier to resolve. We will discuss each weakness, referring back to the illustration of the traditional accounting process (Figure 2–3) throughout the discussion.

Weakness 1. *Stored data have limited characteristics about transactions.*

The data captured in the traditional accounting system are only a subset of the descriptive data about business events. The process captures primarily the date and financial impact of a subset of business events. Date, account, and amount are all you need to produce financial statements, but that is inadequate from the enterprise perspective to plan, control, and evaluate the organization.

We already mentioned the observations of Robert Eccles in Chapter 1 regarding changes in the nature of measurements management is requesting to manage the organization. The limited dimensions recorded in traditional

---

[6]See both of the following references for a detailed analysis of McCarthy's initial work on the data-related aspects of accounting systems:

W.E. McCarthy, "The REA Accounting Model: A Generalized Framework for Accounting Systems in a Shared Data Environment," *The Accounting Review*, July 1982, pp. 554–77.

_____, "The Entity-Relationship View of Accounting Models," *The Accounting Review*, October 1979, pp. 667–86.

FIGURE 2-8

Eight Weaknesses of Traditional Accounting Systems

1. Stored data has limited characteristics about transactions.

2. Data classification schemes are not always appropriate or supportive.

3. Aggregation level of stored data is too high.

4. Useful integration of financial and nonfinancial data across the organization is difficult, if not impossible.

5. Recording, maintaining, and reporting processes seriously limit the system's ability to provide timely support for decision makers.

6. Traditional processing methods are not well adapted to changing business requirements.

7. Implementing and maintaining internal controls are costly, ineffective, and not performed in a timely manner.

8. Antiquated processing and storage methods are costly to maintain and operate.

---

accounting systems don't provide the multidimensional view being requested by today's information customers, including investors, creditors, unions, consumer groups, regulators, and governments. Without a more complete description of business events, information customers are constrained in their ability to plan, control, or evaluate business processes of the organization.

Weakness 2. *Data classification schemes are not always appropriate or supportive.*

A second weakness is that a chart of accounts represents the primary means for organizing financial data. Not only must the primary data be financial in nature, they must be classified according to the chart of accounts framework. Maintaining the data in the chart of accounts in summary form precludes alternative views of the data. There is no convenient way for accountants to reclassify or reformat the data. Report flexibility is limited to selecting specific accounts with their account balances. When this is not adequate a myriad of artifacts such as dummy accounts, subsidiary ledgers, and contra accounts may be created to "fix" the chart of accounts.

This weakness focuses on the classification scheme, not the entire accounting process. If your only objective is to present summarized financial statements, then the chart of accounts classification scheme is logical. All that most of our information customers want is useful information about the business events and many are complaining that the traditional classification scheme is confusing at best, and possibly misleading at worst. Part of the reason for this is that the classification scheme often leads to data being classified in a manner that hides its essential nature, especially to nonaccountants who lack a detailed understanding of the accounting process.

By staying with a chart of accounts classification scheme, we are asking users to decide, once and for all, what they want to know about their business so we can set up, once and for all, an appropriate classification scheme. From an accounting point of view it is like saying, "If management would simply run the business like we measure it, there would be no problems." Because there is no one correct view, however, organizations can eventually end up with separate charts of accounts for not only financial accounting, management accounting, and tax accounting, but for manufacturing, marketing, corporate headquarters, and field offices as well.

Whether separate charts of accounts or a finer degree of partitioning the accounts, the impact is the same. Either we attempt to identify a single classification scheme for all information customers or we attempt to hold together a diverse set of classification systems employing large numbers of accountants who have the responsibility of keeping all these systems in sync. We view this as an unachievable and unnecessary objective.

Even if we were successful in developing a chart of accounts that satisfies information customer needs today, the requirements of the information customer constantly change to respond to changes in the economic environment. Changing an organization's chart of accounts is no small task. It is not simply a matter of coming up with a new numbering scheme overnight and using it the next day. Changes in the chart of accounts affect the way information is recorded, posted, and closed to the trial balance as well as the comparability of current transaction data with prior period transactions.

Weakness 3. *Aggregation level of stored data is too high.*

Aggregation refers to the degree to which data are summarized. In the traditional accounting model, transaction data that are initially recorded in a special journal are summarized for a specified period of time (e.g., quarterly, monthly, or weekly). This total is posted to a ledger account and the running ledger account balance is updated. Information customers, whether internal or external, are limited to these levels of aggregation. They can obtain information about individual transactions, totals by transaction types according to the predetermined time periods, and running ledger account balances. Alternative systems must be developed and maintained to provide any other levels of aggregation.

Accounting data are used by a wide variety of decision makers, each needing different quantities, aggregations, and focuses, depending upon their personalities, decision styles, experience, and responsibilities. As Nobel laureate Herbert Simon has observed, decision makers function in a variety of decision environments, each in a unique way. Therefore:

> we must expect to find different systems [people] . . . using quite different strategies to perform the same task. I am not aware that any theorems have been proved about the uniqueness of good, or even best, strategies. Thus, we must expect to find strategy differences not only between systems at different skill levels, but even between experts.[7]

It should not be surprising, therefore, that because individuals have different decision processes they also have different information requirements. The danger in supporting a number of different decision models with a single classification scheme of aggregated data is not only in adopting an inappropriate classification method, but in providing only aggregated data so as to preclude alternative aggregations of the data to meet the requirements of diverse information customers.

This is not to say aggregation is wrong. Rather, we must be cautious about using one particular aggregation method for one information customer which precludes another very different, but equally valid, aggregation for another information customer. We must respect and adapt to the individuality of information customers' decision processes and preferences, while also providing some standard measures of the organization. As you will see in later chapters, the two objectives are not mutually exclusive.

Weakness 4. *Useful integration of financial and nonfinancial data across the organization is difficult, if not impossible.*

---

[7]H. A. Simon, "Cognitive Science: The Newest Science of the Artificial," *Cognitive Science*, January-March 1980, pp. 33–46.

Poor integration of financial and nonfinancial data is the cumulative impact of the first three weaknesses. Unless they are resolved, the best an organization can do is maintain two types of systems: one financial and one nonfinancial. In fact, organizations using the traditional accounting approach maintain both financial and nonfinancial systems. The problem in these cases is that source business-event data is found in the nonfinancial system using one classification scheme with limited financial measurements, while a subset of the business events (accounting transactions) and their financial aspects reside in the financial system with its own classification scheme. As a result, data concerning the same business event is maintained separately by accountants and nonaccountants, thus leading to inconsistencies, information gaps, and overlaps across the organization. The burden is on the information customer to bridge the two systems' processes, classification schemes, and data.

The problem for the organization is the confusion created by the information inconsistencies, gaps, and overlaps. This results in a significant waste for the enterprise due to redundant work which could largely be eliminated. Even in paperless environments like at IBM, a large part of the time spent by the accounting staff is attempting to reconcile financial and non-financial systems.[8] In addition, when decision makers are provided inconsistent, incomplete, or redundant data about a business process, the information is less useful and results in less than optimal decision making.

Because much of what decision makers need to effectively run the business is in the nonfinancial systems, the business is actually run using information outside the accounting system. This raises significant questions concerning the value added by the accounting system.

Let's now examine the four processing weaknesses of traditional accounting systems.

Weakness 5. *The way data is recorded and maintained seriously limits the system's ability to provide timely support for decision makers.*

One of the subtleties of the traditional system is that account balances in the traditional accounting system are never current. Accounting data are generally recorded subsequent to, not simultaneous with, the occurrence of

---

[8]D. P. Andros, J.O. Cherrington, and E.L. Denna, "Reengineer Your Accounting System the IBM Way," *Financial Executive*, July/August 1992, pp. 29-33.

the business event. Accounting entries are typically taken from source documents that were created as part of the business event. The documents are passed to accountants who supervise the data entry in a separate system. Simultaneously recording the event data in the financial system would require business process participants know how to do accounting entries, or accountants would have to be wherever business processes occur. Either alternative is unlikely, unjustifiable, undesirable, and, as we will show, unnecessary.

Another factor preventing timely information is the posting delay. Transaction journal data maintained by accounting professionals is posted to the ledgers anywhere from daily to monthly depending on the organization. Regardless of when the posting occurs, the ledger accounts are always out of date. Even with more frequent posting, accounting reports are typically delivered using a standard schedule like monthly, or bi-weekly at best. Real time accounting data is an impossibility under the traditional system.

The question to ask is, How often are decisions made in an organization? Monthly? Weekly? Decisions occur constantly because information customers are constantly planning, controlling, or evaluating business processes. Therefore, decision makers need current information, constantly. Using the F-15 analogy, not only does the traditional accounting system give limited data to the pilot and its support team, the data is provided only monthly or weekly. Managing without timely information is often called "managing by the wake." The problem is an F-15 and an organization leaves a very long wake after a week's worth of flying. The output from the traditional system is certainly not timely, and must be improved.

Weakness 6. *Traditional processing methods are not very adaptive to changing business requirements.*

The traditional system is much like pouring organizational and strategic cement. Rather than the system enabling continual change in an organization's structure, operations, and strategy, the cost and difficulty of modifying the traditional system often results in formidable resistance to any change, regardless of the business reason for the change. Many organizations that attempt to make their business and information processes more efficient and effective find strong resistance from accountants who cling to traditional methods of organizing, recording, maintaining, and reporting financial information.

This resistance is due to both human nature and the architecture of the traditional accounting system. By resolving the data-related weaknesses, the adaptiveness of the processes becomes far less an issue. However, the behavioral resistance to change is more significant. Some find change exciting and rewarding, others find it terrifying and disconcerting. Many people strongly resist the idea of continual change. Because of its rigid nature, changing the operation of a traditional accounting system makes change all the more painful and difficult. It is not much different with traditional nonfinancial systems as well. Therefore, the rigidity of the traditional system tends to reinforce the resistance of those who would resist change regardless of the need for change or the ability of the system's architecture to change.

Weakness 7. *Implementing and maintaining internal controls are costly, ineffective, and not performed in a timely manner.*

In the traditional accounting process, accountants are not directly involved in the business process, nor are they involved in capturing the actual event data. Because the systems that document business events are not accounting systems, controls over business and information processes are often inadequate. The danger is that decision makers will make decisions using information from nonfinancial systems that is unaudited and lacks appropriate controls. Even when decision makers use accounting information in their decision-making processes the final "Good Housekeeping" seal of approval comes only periodically. Not only is the information not provided in real time, the auditing is even less timely, nearly always occurring after the fact and concentrating on data that is used by a relatively small number of information customers.

The fact is, traditional accounting controls are more detective than preventive. The traditional audit focuses primarily on discovering breaches of control after the fact and recommending corrections to the system or organization structure. With management constantly refining business processes and organization structures, the audit is always one step behind. The accountant maintains a largely detective posture, constantly trying to patch controls in place while the business races on.

By the time a breach in control is detected, the damage is already done. We hope to catch any significant errors or irregularities but fully realize that errors do go undetected. Using primarily detective controls, however, is contrary to good process management which drives toward zero-defect rates. The thought of a tolerable error rate is at odds with this concept. The old adage, "An ounce of prevention is worth a pound of cure," is certainly applicable. Furthermore, all too often the cure is much more expensive than the prevention as we are painfully learning from a variety of business failures. We are left to question the business value of the traditional approach to controlling business and information-processing risk. We can, and must, be more efficient and effective in controlling business and information-processing risk. The problem is the traditional systems architecture contributes only marginally toward achieving such a goal.

Weakness 8. *Antiquated processing and storage methods are costly to maintain and operate.*

Maintaining the traditional financial and nonfinancial systems architecture is unnecessarily expensive. The primary reason for the excessive costs is the unnecessary duplication of data storage and processing throughout the organization. Many organizations spend several times the amount of money needed to maintain a well integrated, cohesive, enterprisewide information system. In a day when organizations face stiff competition and narrow profit margins, the thought of wasting even small amounts of money is unfortunate. Wasting large amounts of money is dangerous.

Some organizations attempt to solve the problem by applying more automation. The weaknesses of traditional accounting systems, particularly the data-related weaknesses, are not resolved by simply making the system faster through automation. Simply applying automation without rethinking the way data is organized and processed cannot resolve these weaknesses. Architecture problems dealing with what is stored, how it is stored, and how it is processed are not resolved by improving the system's efficiency through the use of information technology.

Other than making the process more efficient, automation may exacerbate many of the problems by simply proliferating the traditional architecture throughout the organization. A simple example of an international computer manufacturer which maintains separate charts of accounts for its manufacturing and marketing divisions illustrates this problem. Two ledgers are required because the two divisions have different criteria for reporting financial information. Manufacturing recognizes revenue when a product is shipped to a customer, while marketing recognizes revenue when the customer is billed for the shipped product. The entire accounting process is automated.

Below are the journal entries to record the following transactions:

December 15   Shipped a $300,000 computer to a customer.

January 10   Billed the customer $320,000, adjusting for the features
                added during installation.

On January 3rd, the following entries to record the December 15 transaction are posted to the ledgers as part of the month-end closing and reporting process:

Manufacturing ledger:
    Contra   300,000
        Revenue   300,000
    Trans-12   300,000
        Control   300,000

Marketing ledger:
    Unbilled Accounts Receivable   300,000
        Contra   300,000
    Control   300,000
        Trans-30   300,000

The Contra, Trans, and Control accounts offset one another during the corporate rollup process leaving the simple debit to unbilled accounts receivable and a credit to revenue. Billing occurs on the 10th of each month, but because posting only occurs monthly, the next transaction is posted to the ledger on the 3rd of February.

Marketing ledger:
    Accounts Receivable Billed   320,000
        Contra   320,000
    Control   320,000
        Trans-30   320,000

Manufacturing ledger:
    Contra   320,000
        Revenue   320,000
    Trans-12   320,000
        Control   320,000

The problem at this point is that $620,000 has been recognized as revenue, not $320,000. To correct for this the original entries are reversed as follows:

Manufacturing ledger:
Revenue	300,000	
Contra		300,000
Control	300,000	
Trans-12		300,000

Marketing ledger:
Contra	300,000	
Unbilled Accounts Receivable		300,000
Trans-30	300,000	
Control		300,000

A total of 24 entries are used to record two simple accounting transactions! This does not take into account subsequent discounts, currency exchange rates, billing adjustments, or the possibility of value added taxes for crossing international boundaries. You can see that such an architecture is both cumbersome and costly. Furthermore, you should be able to see why the hope of a real-time reporting environment using the traditional architecture is unrealistic, particularly as an organization grows and its business and information requirements become more complex. The traditional architecture creates a nearly impossible balancing act for both accounting and IT professionals. It is not difficult for the architecture to quickly get out of hand in promulgating hundreds of different ledger and subledger systems to accommodate the variety of information and processing requirements across an organization.[9]

Our discussion and examples are focused around accounting systems and the architecture that supports them. But the weaknesses we noted in the traditional accounting system can be generalized to many nonfinancial systems in which data is captured and stored specific to a narrow functional view instead of an organizationwide perspective.

Our criticism of the traditional accounting process is not intended to say that Pacioli proposed the wrong concepts or process, or that what we have done for the past 400 years is wrong or worthless. *We are only saying we now*

---

[9]Ibid, pp. 28–31.

have the opportunity and the need to rethink the architecture of both financial and nonfinancial systems. Pacioli's world was very different from ours. His was a world characterized by comparatively simple business organizations, simple information requirements by a small number of information customers (primarily proprietors), simple and stable markets for goods/services, simple capital markets (if they existed at all), and a simple information technology.

We feel Pacioli's original ideas were nothing short of brilliant in terms of proposing a method for recording, maintaining, and reporting economic data with a fairly primitive information technology (quill, inkwell, and parchment). However, today's economic world makes it imperative that we rethink the basic architecture of both financial and nonfinancial systems. Moreover, today's technology makes it possible.

As we noted in Chapter One, Thomas Johnson and Robert Kaplan observe:

> The challenge and the opportunity for contemporary organizations . . . is clear . . . systems can and should be designed to support the operations and the strategy of the organization. The technology exists to implement systems radically different from those being used today. What is lacking is knowledge. But this knowledge can emerge from experimentation and communication.[10]

The solution centers around developing a single architecture which allows us to focus on the fundamental business problems of fixing inefficient and ineffective business processes, unnecessary and burdensome organization structures, inadequate measurements to guide management, and ineffective uses of information technology. The details of this thrust rest upon what we call event-driven solution concepts.

CONCEPTS FOR SOLVING THE PROBLEM

We have identified five key concepts that are necessary in resolving the eight weaknesses. As we mentioned in Chapter One, these concepts have been identified as a result of analyzing our own, and others', successful efforts to solve business problems. The five solution concepts include:

---

[10]H. T. Johnson, and R. S. Kaplan, *Relevance Lost: The Rise and Fall of Management Accounting,* (Boston: Harvard Business School Press, 1987), pp. 17-18.

1. Focus on business events.
2. Simplify business processes.
3. Integrate data.
4. Integrate information processes and controls.
5. Realign system component ownership.

The following section provides some more details about each of these solution concepts.

Focus on Business Events

A business event represents any business activity that management wants to plan, control, and evaluate. Conversely, accounting transactions represent a subset of business events. Focusing on business events redefines the scope of accounting. Rather than selecting only business events that change the company's assets, liabilities, or owner's equity, we select those business events that management wants to plan, control, and evaluate. This focus automatically forces an integration of the functional areas of an enterprise and enables the integration of both financial and nonfinancial data.

The business events orientation makes the business event, whether economic or noneconomic, the fundamental unit of analysis rather than an information artifact.[11] The focus is on understanding which business events are essential to the organization, how the organization operates, and how it could operate, rather than on the function of the current information system, or the lack thereof. The goal is to build a system that actually describes and supports the organization and its operations so that the architecture of the system (its data and processes) is intuitive to all information customers. If you look once again at the illustration of the traditional accounting system, the processes and data do not describe the nature of business processes. As a result, even though someone may know their business process inside and out, they do not understand the operation and use of the accounting process. This inevitably inhibits their use of the accounting system and its output. They must learn how accountants think to understand the output. If, however, the system was a reflection of the business, such a problem would not exist.

---

[11]An information artifact is any man-made creation of data or process. The traditional chart of accounts or journalizing and posting processes are examples of information artifacts. For that matter, any existing system is an information artifact.

Simplify Business Processes

In his article "Re-engineering Work: Don't Automate, Obliterate," published by the *Harvard Business Review*, Michael Hammer points out that although U.S. companies have made tremendous strides in restructuring and downsizing, most are still unprepared to operate in the 1990s. Efforts to streamline and automate outdated processes have not yielded the dramatic improvements required to compete despite enormous investments in IT. The problem is such investments are made to simply mechanize old ways of doing business. Automation, therefore, simply speeds up, rather than fixes, outdated processes.

> It is time to stop paving the cow paths. Instead of embedding outdated processes in silicon and software, we should obliterate them and start over. We should "re-engineer" our businesses: use the power of modern information technology to radically redesign our business processes in order to achieve dramatic improvements in their performance.[12]

Experience has proven over and over again that simply automating inherently inadequate processes and architectures will not solve their inherent problems. Therefore, we must rethink processes and then apply IT.

Integrate Data

Data integration focuses on organizing all relevant data about all business events into one logical information store instead of having a series of loosely integrated systems which often have information gaps and overlaps (e.g., the financial/nonfinancial paradigm). This single integrated store of data supporting all information customer views about business events forms the foundation of the enterprise information warehouse, an oft overused media term which typically means a big database. However, simply applying database technology to an inadequate data architecture is not the solution. The key to data integration is focusing on what is represented by the data (the business events) not on information customer views (e.g., financial statements, management reports, or regulatory reports). Information customer requirements can change radically over time. But, organizing data to reflect

---

[12]M. Hammer, "Re-engineering Work: Don't Automate, Obliterate," *Harvard Business Review*, July-August 1990, p. 104.

the essential nature of the business (its business events) provides both a stable and flexible architecture.

Integrate Information Processes and Controls

With an integrated enterprise information warehouse in place, attention can turn to information process integration and building in controls over both the business and information processes. Without an integrated enterprise information warehouse, the goal of significant process integration is not possible. As soon as business data is partitioned between financial and nonfinancial data (or any other type of partition) the number of processes quickly multiplies. Not only do you have to have two sets of recording, maintenance, and reporting processes, you need processes to reconcile the separate systems as well.

Process integration focuses on integrating the functional requirements of the three essential information activities—recording, maintaining, and reporting—and the controls required in each to address the related business and information processing risk. Particularly important is the integration of all requirements relevant to the recording of event data. In addition, process integration focuses on embedding the system into the actual business process itself so that the use of information technology to perform the business process actually results in the event data being recorded while the business process occurs.

The trick is utilizing information technology to both simplify the business and information processes while building in effective controls. A good example of this approach is work performed at United Parcel Service (UPS). During 1991, UPS implemented penpoint technology to support the business process of delivering packages. Rather than writing the package and address information on a clipboard, all information about the package and delivery address is stored in a central computer and then downloaded to the portable computer each day. When customers sign for the package they do so directly on the computer itself using an electronic pen. All information about each delivery event (e.g., the package delivered, the delivery person, the recipient, the time and date of delivery, and the signature) is recorded and then transmitted via cellular radio to UPS headquarters as often as is cost justified. As a result, anyone needing information about the delivery of packages can look at a single store of information that is recorded in one single process.

The proper integration of processes can result in significant savings to the organization and can facilitate significant re-engineering of both business and information processes. One of the benefits of process integration is the identification of clerical processes which can potentially be automated, thereby shifting human resources toward nonmechanical, decision-oriented tasks.

Realign System Component Ownership

The full realization of the prior four solution concepts is dependent on resolving some significant and longstanding problems regarding the ownership of systems and data. Because this is such an important issue, we will discuss this concept in a little more detail in this chapter. The other solution concepts will be discussed at length throughout the remainder of the book.

Event-driven business solutions have three primary components (see Figure 2–9):

> Recording and maintenance processes—the specific procedures used to capture and update business event data.
>
> Data—the data captured and maintained by the recording and maintenance procedures that form the enterprise-wide data base.
>
> Reporting processes—the procedures used to generate the information (views) required by various information customers (both internal and external).

When these three components are combined, they form what we refer to as a business solution, not just an IT application. Traditionally, the need for an application arises when information is needed by an individual or a group, or when a business or information process is amenable to automation. Those needing the information pay for developing and operating the desired application.

Information system ownership traditionally resides at the application level. Each application owner owns all data and related processes. Interaction among related applications is subject to the ability and desire of application owners to cooperate with one another. A problem results when someone other than the application owner needs to combine data maintained by one or more applications with other data to produce a new report. There are two solutions when this occurs: first, modify the reporting capabilities of the existing

FIGURE 2-9

Business Event-Driven Solution Components

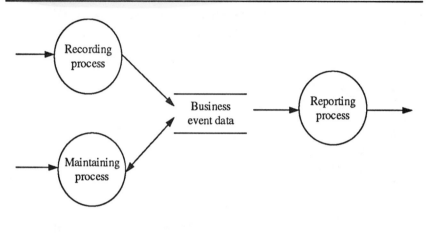

applications to meet the unmet demands; or, second, give the needed data to those requesting it and have them develop their own applications to meet their own reporting requirements.

Because nonapplication owners' needs are secondary to those of the application owner, modification requests typically are given less attention, if they are considered at all. Instead, data is typically passed to the nonapplication owner to be reprocessed to meet the new information need. From an enterprise perspective, this causes needless duplication in recording, maintaining, and reporting organization data and foils efforts to integrate data and processes across the enterprise. The architecture of the system resembles that of a bowl of spaghetti. Obviously, this is not an optimal solution.

When the focus is on developing event-driven business solutions, all information needs relating to each business event are considered simultaneously and are integrated into a single enterprise information model. Thus, the needs of one individual do not dominate the needs of others. Therefore, until the information system component ownership issue is resolved, the likelihood of successfully creating and implementing event-driven business solutions is quite low, if not impossible.

We suggest the following principles for dividing system component ownership and responsibilities:

Principle 1. *The enterprise owns all data.* When the enterprise assumes ownership of all data, it also assumes responsibility to:

1. Integrate the variety of information needs (individual views) for each event into an integrated enterprise information model.
2. Specify the types of data to be recorded and maintained about each business event.
3. Provide information customers with the necessary tools to meet reporting requirements across the organization.
4. Ensure that the recording, maintenance, and reporting processes have adequate controls.
5. Coordinate and oversee the development of both the technological platform as well as the business process solutions.

This is a significant departure from traditional concepts of data ownership. However, making this move is critical to applying the prior solution concepts.

Principle 2. *Responsibility for recording and maintaining business event data lies with those responsible for planning, executing, and controlling business events.* Once reporting requirements have been considered and an enterprise data model has been specified, responsibility for recording and maintaining business event data can be specified. Ideally, business event data are all recorded in real time during the execution of the business event. The recorded data can then be accessed by any authorized information customer. In order to record and maintain business event data while the event occurs, responsibility for recording and maintaining business event data logically resides with the business event owner.

Principle 3. *Individual information customers are responsible for extracting the information they need for their decision-making purposes.* The enterprise should facilitate extracting information by providing information customers with the tools needed for both planned and ad hoc queries. Giving information customers responsibility for extracting their own information will result in the need for training in the use of the query tools provided by the organization.

To summarize the ownership concepts, data ownership must reside with the enterprise as a whole to integrate the variety of views of business events. No one information view should dominate the type or method of data storage and processing. This can only be administered at the enterprise level.

Similarly, recording and maintaining business event data logically resides with those responsible for managing the business event. Finally, information customers are responsible for their specific uses of the enterprise data. Without such a division of responsibilities, organizations will find significant resistance to the development of business solutions that have an enterprise perspective.

The effect of the five solution concepts is the creation of business solutions built on the architecture illustrated in Figure 2–10. The architecture is characterized by business event data being gathered and passed through a business event processor that executes all relevant business and information process rules. The data is then stored in an integrated repository that is available to any authorized enterprise information customer through a reporting facility. Those familiar with client-server architecture will recognize how closely the solution concepts support this increasingly popular and powerful philosophy.

FIGURE 2-10

Event-Driven Business Solution Architecture

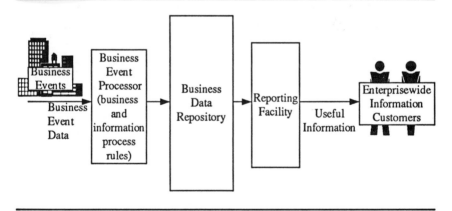

APPLYING THE SOLUTION CONCEPTS

Can the solution be so simple? Again, we caution you against confusing conceptual simplicity and elegance with ease of implementation. Although we have found the concepts make developing business solutions better, faster, and cheaper, initiating any kind of change in business processes, organization structure, the use of IT, or business measurements is challenging. Implementing these solution concepts requires leadership by executives with the courage to challenge old assumptions and establish a new order of things. The remainder of this book focuses on each of the solution concepts and provides greater detail regarding the definition and implementation of each.

Chapter Three

Business Events
*What Are They and How Do They
Enable the Development of Business
Solutions?*

AN EVENT PERSPECTIVE

Imagine that a salesperson for a large computer manufacturer sells 2,000 computers to a wealthy retail magnate. How many different views are there of this one simple business event? That depends on who wants to know about new customer orders. Let's list just a few of the possibilities:

Production personnel want to know about the order to plan production processes.

Marketing wants to know about the order to possibly adjust prices, plan advertising, and target future sales efforts.

Personnel wants to know about the order to pay sales commissions.

Executive management wants to know about the order to plan, control, and evaluate its impact on the organization.

Investors and creditors want to know about orders to assess the profitability of their investments and the likelihood of returns on their investment.

Not only is there a variety of different information customers interested in knowing about the order, each view of the order is different. Each class of information customers wants to know something a bit different from the others. The notion of multiple information views of the same phenomena is illustrated in Figure 3–1.

Traditionally, we have addressed this diversity by building a different system for each view. Each system captures slightly different data about the same business event, each selecting its own subset of available data about the

FIGURE 3-1
Information Customer Views

Personnel view

Production view

Business event
(sale)

Marketing view

Executive view

Investors and creditors view

event and recording it in its own classification scheme. However, by changing our orientation toward business events, we focus on that which underlies the wide variety of information customer views. This prevents the need for multiple systems which overlap each other and the duplication of work. As Peter Drucker points out, the variety of systems (both financial and nonfinancial):

> increasingly overlap. They also increasingly come up with what look like conflicting—or at least incompatible—data about the same event; for the two look at the same event quite differently. Till now this has created little confusion. Companies tended to pay attention to what their accountants told them and to disregard the data of their information system, at least for top-management decisions. But this is changing as computer-literate executives are moving into decision-making positions.[1]

---

[1]P. Drucker, "Be Data Literate—Know What to Know," *The Wall Street Journal*, December 1, 1992, p. C1.

Anyone who has tried to reconcile the data that support the alternative views across an organization understands what we mean by conflicting views. Reconciling differences among the conflicting views is difficult at best and occasionally impossible. Any reconciliation achieved is destroyed as soon as one or more of the views change. The important point here is that these seemingly irreconcilable and diverse classification schemes (views) are simply alternative ways of looking at the same phenomena—business events.

If we capture the essential characteristics of business events without favoring any particular classification scheme, we can support an infinite number of views of the data with a single description. With the fundamental characteristics of business events in hand, we can generate any number of current views (e.g., financial statements, management reports, and regulatory reports) and also develop entirely new views to respond to changing information customer requirements. Furthermore, we can help respond to the challenges facing organizations which we introduced in Chapter One: inefficient and ineffective business processes, unnecessary and burdensome organization structure, inadequate measurements to guide management, ineffective uses of information technology. The question is, "What are the business events and what are the essential characteristics to capture about business events?"

ESSENTIAL CHARACTERISTICS OF BUSINESS EVENTS

Business events are the essential organization activities that management wants to plan, control, and evaluate in order to achieve its business objectives. Examples of business events include:

Receiving a customer order.

Shipping merchandise.

Collecting customer payments.

One error often made in identifying business events is confusing information processes with business events. The relationship between the two is fairly simple—business events trigger information processes (Figure 3–2). For example, a customer order (the business event) triggers information processes to record business event data and confirm the order. Although the difference seems rather straightforward, many struggle to distinguish the two.

FIGURE 3-2
Relationship Between Business Events and Information Processes

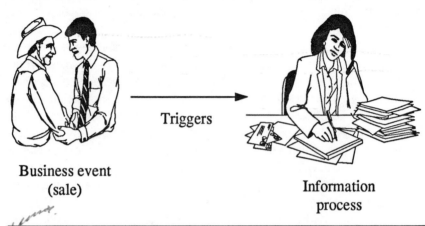

Triggers

Business event
(sale)

Information
process

Information processes are activities that utilize a variety of information technologies to record data about business events; maintain reference information about the resources, agents, and locations involved in business events; and report information to information customers so they can plan, control, or evaluate business processes and events.

Since this is such an important concept, let's look at a few examples in order to illustrate the difference between business events and information processes. The delivery of a product to a customer is an example of a business event; recording data about the delivery is an information process. Receiving a payment from a customer for goods and services provided is a business event; recording data about the customer payment is an information process. Therefore, generating financial statements, invoices, checks, management reports, regulatory reports, or any other reports are information processes. Without accounting information those planning, controlling, and evaluating business events have little to guide their efforts. However, when the focus is on managing financial statements as opposed to managing business events, you risk missing the mark and sub-optimizing your business.

By focusing on the essence of the business process and building an information system to support it we are reversing the process typically followed. Historically, systems have been developed to satisfy a reporting requirement. The process began with identifying the format of the report, defining the classification scheme, then accumulating and summarizing the necessary event data. Often this data would be found in a variety of existing systems which would require the development of some kind of interface with upstream applications. As a result, the simplicity of the view/event relationship became lost in a morass of poorly coordinated systems which were collectively difficult to operate and nearly impossible to modify.

If we attempt to apply IT by first focusing on the reports and classification schemes, the proverbial tail (classification scheme) wags the dog (business events)—accounting and IT professionals try to get business processes to adapt to the information processes and classification schemes. When the report or the classification scheme changes, the way the system processes data is out of date and requires rework. We avoid this problem when we focus on identifying, capturing, and processing the essential characteristics of that which underlies the numerous views across an organization—the business events.

Much of the theory supporting the identification of the essential characteristics of business events was first proposed by Bill McCarthy,[2] an accounting systems scholar studying the organization of business data for multiple classification schemes. During the early 1980s, McCarthy proposed a generalized model to guide the development of a single repository of business data. McCarthy demonstrated that by capturing the essential characteristics of a business event, an infinite number of classification schemes can be supported, including traditional accounting information. Our experience has shown that McCarthy's model provides a reliable means for identifying the essential characteristics of business events.

Any information customer requirement relates to the following five questions about each business event:

What happened and when? The "what" identifies which business event occurred and the "when" describes the order of the events, what time the event started, and the time it ended. Often it is also important to know how long it took for the event to transpire. For example, when cleaning a carpet, performing an audit, performing open heart surgery, turning a part on a lathe,

---

[2]See W. E. McCarthy, "The REA Accounting Model: A Generalized Framework for Accounting Systems in a Shared Data Environment," *The Accounting Review*, July 1982, pp. 554–77, for a complete description of the underlying theory.

or a myriad of other business events, we must know the length of time for the individual events in order to effectively plan, control, and evaluate them.

What roles were played and who/what performed the roles? We must know what roles were performed and who/what performed them. Roles can range from internal responsibilities (e.g., salesperson, cleaning person, supervisor, or inspector) to external roles (e.g., customer or supplier). These roles can be performed by individuals, organizations, or programmable machines (such as robots or computers). Those performing roles are referred to as agents. Events involving the exchange of resources between organizations always involve both internal and external agents, each performing a different role during the execution of the event. For example, the internal role of a salesperson may be performed by a person or a computer terminal which interacts with someone or something playing the external role (customer). Whether the event involves the exchange of resources or not, we must capture data about the roles played and the agents involved. This information is critical to support those planning, controlling, and evaluating business events.

What kinds of resources were involved and how much was used? All business events involve the use of one or more resources. We must also know the type and quantity of resources involved in each event. Identifying and measuring some resources is fairly straightforward, while others are not. For example, a sale of groceries (the resource) is easily measured. However, we could also argue that several other resources are involved (e.g., the cash register, bags to package the groceries, and electricity to power the cash register) which are much more difficult to measure. At what point do you stop identifying the type and quantity of resources? It depends on the preferences of those planning, controlling, and evaluating the business events. Regardless of the level of detail, we must have information about the type and quantity of resources involved in each event.

Where did the event occur? Lastly, we must know where events occur. With today's organizations and information technology spread all over the globe, events can occur anywhere and the customer need not be physically present. To the extent that it is important, we should make sure data about the location of an event are captured. Sometimes the location of the event is embedded in the location of the agents or resources involved. However, when the event location is not derivable by association with the resources or agents, we must explicitly specify the event location.

The important point to emphasize is the impact of recording the essential characteristics of business events and making them available for information customers across the organization. Once the essential data about the event is recorded, we can support an infinite number of information customer views.

BUSINESS PROCESSES AND EVENTS

Although the definition of a business event is rather straightforward, starting the process of identifying business events may seem a bit nebulous at first. The process becomes easier when you divide the business into distinct processes. At the most fundamental level, every organization, regardless of its purpose, goods and services, location, or ownership, has three basic business processes:

Acquisition/payment process.

Conversion process.

Sales/collections process.

Let's take a look at each one in turn.

Acquisition/Payment Process

The acquisition/payment process includes the business events involved in acquiring, paying for, and maintaining the goods and services needed by the organization. The focus is on purchasing only what is needed and can be paid for, receiving only what is ordered, paying for only that which is received, and making sure the resources acquired are available when needed. Organizations acquire a wide variety of goods and services including:

✓ Human resources (e.g., people's time and skills).

✓ Financial resources.

✓ Supplies.

- Inventories.

- ✓ Property, plant, and equipment.
- ✓ New ideas (e.g., research and development).
- ✓ Miscellaneous services (e.g., legal, power, telephone, protection, medical, financial, and custodial).

Regardless of the type of goods and services, each causes only minor alterations in the nature of the process. The more common types of acquisition/payment processes are those for human resources (personnel/payroll processing), financial resources, inventories, and fixed assets.

The basic nature of the process, regardless of the type of resource being acquired, has the following types of events:

> *Request* the good or service.
>
> *Select* a supplier.
>
> *Order* the good or service.
>
> *Receive* the good or service.
>
> *Inspect* the good or service.
>
> *Pay* for the good or service.

If you think through the events in the process carefully, you will notice some organizations may order the events differently, may use a subset of the events, or may add more detailed events. Nonetheless, the basic nature of the process is fairly stable across organizations and resources.

Conversion Process

The conversion process focuses on developing and executing the most efficient and effective processes for converting goods and services acquired into goods and resources for sale. Conversion processes across, or even within, organizations are very diverse and depend on the type of good or service being produced, the technology and resources utilized, the restrictions of regulators, governments, society, or customers, and the preferences of management. Some of the more general types of conversion processes include:

> Assembling.
>
> Growing.

Excavating. *Recruiting*

Harvesting.

Basic manufacturing (e.g., metals, woods, and chemicals).

Finished manufacturing (e.g., tools, instruments, and components).

Cleaning. *Developing*

Transporting.

Distributing.

Providing (e.g., power, water, protection, and communication).

Educating. *orientation*

Discovering (e.g., research and development).

The diversity of conversion processes makes it difficult to propose a single generalized conversion process. Assembling a toy car is vastly different from defending a client in court or discovering a cure for a crippling disease. Furthermore, any one organization may utilize more than one type of conversion process to generate unique goods and services for customers. Nonetheless, at the heart of any conversion process is a sequence of business events which serves to convert goods and services acquired into goods and services for customers.

Sales/Collections Process

The sales/collection process includes the sequence of events involved in exchanging goods and services with customers for payment. Essentially, the sales/collection process is the mirror image of the acquisition/payment process. Whenever one organization or individual acquires and pays for goods and services someone else is selling the good or service and receiving payment. Although there is some diversity across the types of goods and services sold, the basic process typically involves the following events:

- *Receive* an order for goods or services.
- *Select* the good or service to be delivered.
- *Inspect* the good or service to be delivered.
- *Prepare* the good or service for delivery.
- *Deliver* the good or service.

Receive payment for the good or service.

As with the acquisition/payment process, some organizations may order the events differently, may use a subset of the events, or may add more detailed events. Regardless, the basic nature of the process remains intact.

Business events and processes are related because a business process is a sequence of business events. Once a business process has been identified, we can begin decomposing the process into a sequence of discrete business events that management wants to plan, control, and evaluate. One frequently asked question is, "How far do you go when decomposing business processes into business events?"

Decomposing Business Events

The extent to which business processes should be decomposed into business events is fairly simple to determine. Decompose the processes to the level that management wants to plan, control, and evaluate. Each business process is composed of a series of discrete business events. For example, selling mail-order merchandise might involve the following business events:

Accept customer order.

Select, inspect, and package merchandise.

Ship merchandise.

Receive customer payment.

However, someone may rationally argue that the process really involves just two events:

Ship merchandise.

Receive payment.

So which is right? Again, the answer depends on the level of detail at which management wants to plan, control, and evaluate the business process. Because of the diversity of management styles, resource availability, and employee talent, differences will exist across enterprises regarding the level at which organizations manage business processes. Instances will exist in which the sequence of events within the same process in two different organization is reversed. For example, some organizations may insist on the following sequence:

Receive payment.

Ship merchandise.

The sequence of events may be a function of the technique for achieving an objective. For example, constructing a building begins with excavation work and laying the foundation. Then the building can be framed, siding put in place, plumbing and electrical systems installed, drywall hung, and so forth until the building is completed. In this case construction techniques and laws of nature determine the event sequence.

Sometimes the sequence of events is dictated by customer preference. For example, suppose a car dealership operates in four different cities several miles apart. Customers visit the lots and order cars which may be on other lots. Initially, customers are told to drive to the other lot to pick up the car. However, because many customers are unwilling to drive to the other lot they cancel their orders. Astute business people will realize something needs to change to stop losing customers. Therefore, rather than make the customer pick up the car at another lot, they instigate a new business event called "Transport Car." This requires an employee to drive the ordered car to the lot nearest the customer or even to the customer's house. Adding a Transport Car event is management's attempt to meet the customer needs and have the information they want to plan, control, and evaluate the event.

Because of the nature of these three basic business processes (acquisition/ payment, conversion, and sales/collection) and their interrelationships, an organization can accurately be characterized as a system that acquires inputs, processes the inputs into outputs, and sells the outputs to customers (see Figure 3–3). This is a helpful characterization because we can begin to model the entire organization, its processes and events, using some rather simple modeling techniques. These models enhance communications among those responsible for solving business problems.

MODELING BUSINESS EVENTS

Shifting the focus of the modeling effort from modeling information views and information processes to modeling business events and business processes facilitates communication between businesspeople and business solution professionals. One effective modeling technique for doing this is REAL business modeling.

FIGURE 3-3
Organization as a System

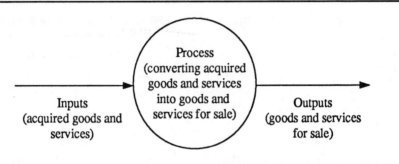

REAL Business Process Modeling

REAL business process modeling is a formal method of representing the essential characteristics of business processes and events. The title REAL is an acronym for Resources, Events, Agents, and Locations which collectively describe the essential characteristics of business processes and events. Event-driven business modeling was first proposed by Bill McCarthy to formalize his concepts regarding the essential nature of business processes and events.[3] Developing a REAL model of business events involves the following steps:

Step 1. Identify business events. The first task in REAL business modeling is to become familiar with the business process and its underlying events. The focus is on identifying the activities management wants to plan, control, and evaluate making sure not to confuse business events with information processes. Figure 3–4 provides a list of the business events commonly found in a mail order company's sales/collection process.

Step 2. Represent the events as boxes. REAL business models are started by identifying the events. Figure 3–5 shows a REAL business essence model at this point. Once the business events have been represented, the next step is to represent the related agents, resources, and locations.

---

[3]Ibid, pp. 554–77.

FIGURE 3-4
Sales/Collection Process Business Events for a Mail Order Business

Customer Places Order

Ship Merchandise

Receive Payment

FIGURE 3-5
1st Stage REAL Business Model for a Mail Order Business
Sales/Collection Process

Customer Places Order

Ship Merchandise

Receive Payment

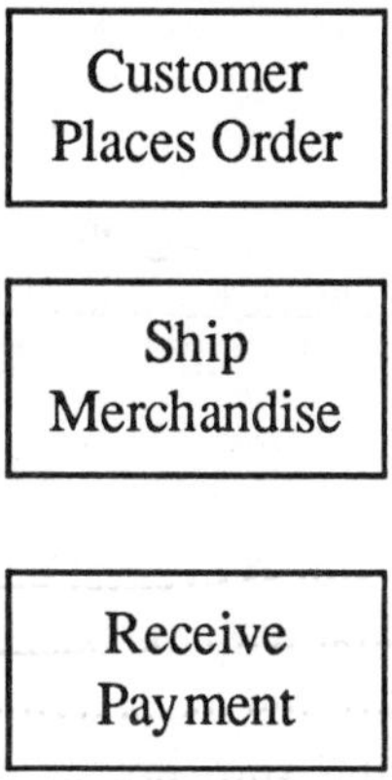

Step 3. Include the relationships among events, agents, resources, and locations. Relating the appropriate agents, resources, and locations to business events describes much of the essential nature of the business process. Agents are the people or machines that execute the business event. There are two types of agents: internal agents and external agents. Internal agents are typically employees who play roles and perform responsibilities within an organization. Internal agents include salespeople, cashiers, manufacturing line workers, and buyers. Sometimes roles can be performed by a machine rather than people. For example:

The ATM machines now play the role traditionally filled by a teller in dispersing and receiving cash.

Robots now play the role of assembly workers traditionally filled by people.

Order entry machines at fast-food stores now play the role of a customer service representative.

Touch sensitive direction systems now play the role of a traffic guide in identifying the most efficient route to get from a rental car agency to a hotel.

In each case, IT is being used to play a role that may have previously been filled by a person. Therefore, it is essential to identify the role being played by internal agents when modeling the essential nature of business processes and events.

External agents are individuals and organizations with whom the organization exchanges goods and services or with whom the organization must interact. Some of the more obvious external agents include customers and suppliers.

Resources vary from being physical to conceptual. Physical resources include the physical plant and equipment of an organization (e.g., buildings, land, equipment, supplies, and inventories). Conceptual resources include employee skills, services the company provides or purchases, or patents and copyrights, and financial resources (which are represented by currency, stock certificates, or bonds). All business events use organization resources either directly or indirectly. If it is difficult to identify a resource with an event, the event is probably unnecessary or adds little value. An accurate REAL business model must identify any significant resources related to an event.

In a REAL business model, resources, agents, and locations are represented by creating a rectangular box for each type of agent and resource and connecting the agent and resource boxes to the event boxes with a line. Figure 3–6 shows an example of a REAL business model with the addition of the resources, events, agents, and locations. For analysis and validation, the resources and locations are typically placed on the left side of events and the agents are on the right side. We have found this approach tends to increase the understanding of the model.

Step 4. Validate the REAL business essence model with the businessperson. Once an initial draft of the REAL business essence model

Resources & Locations on the left *Agents*

FIGURE 3-6
Complete REAL Business Model for a Mail Order Sales/Collection Process

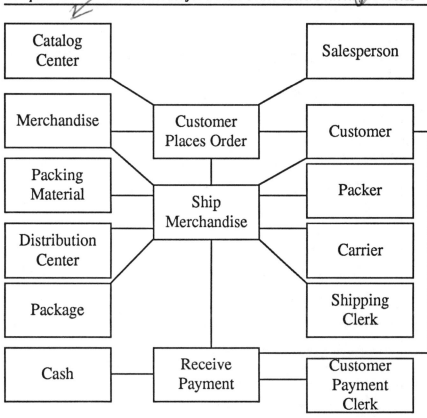

Catalog Center		Salesperson
Merchandise	Customer Places Order	Customer
Packing Material	Ship Merchandise	Packer
Distribution Center		Carrier
Package		Shipping Clerk
Cash	Receive Payment	Customer Payment Clerk

is completed, the next step is to validate the model's adequacy with businesspeople. The validation should be performed by those who understand the details and objectives of the business process and events being modeled and management's objectives concerning planning, controlling, and evaluating the business process. Validation sessions should result in either the confirmation of the model's adequacy or modification of the model.

Modifications typically involve decomposing one or more business events into more detailed business events. For example, in the mail-order sales/ collection example, the Ship Merchandise event may be decomposed to three events (Inspect Merchandise, Package Merchandise, and Ship Merchandise) as shown in Figure 3–7. The choice to decompose to a lower level of detail is determined by management. The justification for additional decomposition is management's information needs to effectively plan, control, and evaluate the business process.

Only a few simple concepts are required to begin developing fairly precise models of business processes and events. The REAL business model serves as a template or pattern of business events which can accelerate both

FIGURE 3-7
REAL Business Model of Sales/Collection Process for Mail Order Company—Decomposed to Lower Level

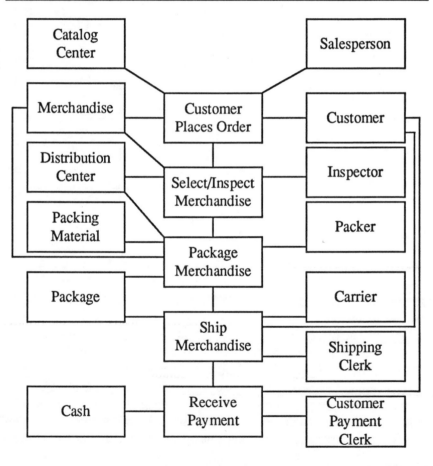

modeling and evaluating business processes. It facilitates identifying and communicating business essence between a businessperson and the analyst. Furthermore, the REAL business model provides a basis for defining the data requirements of a solution, as we will illustrate later in the book.

Obviously, larger, more complex organizations have larger, more complex models of their business processes. However, the essence of the model, no matter how large, rests upon identifying and relating enterprise resources, events, agents, and locations. In fact, the REAL business process model provides a conceptual basis for developing extended enterprise models which span traditional organization boundaries. Such models are becoming more and more common as organizations develop closer ties with vendors and customers and begin sharing both information and processes common to the organizations.

Regardless of the scope, the fundamental unit of analysis is the business event—everything revolves around accurately identifying and describing business events. Identifying business events rests upon what management needs to effectively plan, control, and evaluate their business.

THE CONTRIBUTION OF MODELING BUSINESS EVENTS

Focusing on business processes and events is a fundamental shift in direction over traditional efforts to apply IT. We will address the impact on business structure later. For now we will focus on the impact of applying IT.

Overall, the event focus helps resolve some of the fundamental problems inherent in traditional development processes. Specifically, the event orientation helps develop business solutions in the following significant ways.

First, modeling the business processes and events helps the information professional understand the business. We have already noted the priority understanding business processes has among today's IT professionals. What is lacking is a conceptual foundation for studying business events that leads directly to the development of business solutions. The REAL modeling approach provides this conceptual foundation.

Second, REAL business events modeling keeps the businessperson involved in the solution development process. It helps prevent development efforts from becoming sidetracked or entrenched in complicated development methodologies that lose the interest and attention of businesspeople. As a result, the likelihood of consistent support for, and success of the development effort increases dramatically.

Third, REAL business modeling makes the solution development process more efficient and effective. Traditionally, development efforts have required substantial amounts of time and resources. Often, development efforts drag on to months and years, thereby endangering the support and involvement of business people.

Our experience with REAL business modeling has shown that focusing on business events greatly enhances the likelihood of developing better business solutions. These solutions address everything from changing the way the processes are managed to how IT is utilized. Focusing on business events is the first of the five solution concepts introduced in Chapter Two. It represents the fundamental unit of analysis for developing business solutions and has a significant influence on the remaining solution concepts of this book.

Chapter Four

Business and Information Process Reengineering

Simplifying the Business, Controlling Risk, and Facilitating Continual Improvement of Business and Information Processes.

REENGINEERING: THE LATEST CRAZE

The second solution concept focuses on simplifying business processes. Other titles occasionally used to describe this concept include process simplification, business transformation, total quality management, or business restructuring. Regardless of the title it is given, reengineering has recently become a very popular theme in the press. It seems everyone is on the reengineering bandwagon. Why? Today's business world demands significant changes in business processes, people's responsibilities, the use of technology, and the way we measure business results. In its broadest sense, simplifying business processes embraces a variety of topics aimed at making business and information processes as effective and efficient as possible.

An important element of reengineering is the concept that reengineering is not a one time fix, but a constant reevaluation to improve business and information processes. The focus on continual improvement enables the organization to continually respond to rapidly changing business requirements.

Another important point is that IT enables reengineering, not drives it. Too often technology is applied to bad processes. The result is an efficient, but bad, process with a much more expensive infrastructure supporting it. The correct sequence puts the principles of reengineering business processes in place first and then looks for opportunities to apply IT.

Reengineering focuses on three issues:

Eliminating nonessential processes or events (particularly those requiring significant human intervention).

Making essential processes as efficient and effective as possible (typically through the use of IT).

Enabling new processes to increase the value of an organization's goods and services to customers (again, typically through the use of IT).

Here are some examples of reengineering in each of these three areas.

Eliminating Nonessential Processes/Events

One of the best examples of eliminating nonessential processes is Ford Motor Company's reengineering of their purchase/payment process. As with many organizations, Ford paid vendors based on the receipt of vendor invoices. This long-established practice of processing invoices is common among nearly all organizations. However, as Ford employees examined invoice processing, they realized vendor invoices simply confirmed what they typically already knew at the time they received the goods or services from the vendor.

Ford eliminated nonessential processes of receiving, examining, and reconciling vendor invoices and now pays vendors based on receipt of goods and services. Ford now asks vendors not to send invoices. As a result, Ford has reduced accounts payable headcount by 75 percent while eliminating nearly all information processing errors. Automating the old process would not have provided the significant improvement associated with rethinking the process from the ground up. By rethinking the process, they were able to provide more useful information to management, simplify the business and information processes, and increase the effectiveness of controls over business and information processes.[1]

Making Essential Processes More Efficient and Effective

A good example of making essential processes more efficient and effective is the work of Dr. David Shepard of Minden, Louisiana.

---

[1]M. Hammer, "Re-engineering Work: Don't Automate, Obliterate," *Harvard Business Review*, July-August 1990, p. 104–12.

You might look elsewhere than rural Minden, La., to find a recently introduced, state-of-the-art, $28,000 medical expert system. Yet, Dr. David Shepard, an internist, is the only doctor in the country who has it. What he has is the PC version of the Medicomp system. Medicomp is an innovative patient-care system for doctors and hospitals that combines expert-system diagnosis of ailments with a near-comprehensive patient-recordkeeping system. The Medicomp system maintains a paperless "electronic chart" on each patient. Data on a patient's background, illnesses, medications, lab tests and physical exams are entered into the system using laser printed scan sheets, which are filled out with No. 2 pencils like standardized scholastic tests. The expert system gives Dr. Shepard second opinions on diagnoses and generates "intelligent scan sheets" that contain questions and tests more specific to individual patients' conditions. Dr. Shepard said the system has increased his income about $2,000 a month by letting him handle more patients and has helped him raise the quality of his care.[2]

As you can see, Dr. Shepard drastically increased the efficiency and effectiveness of essential business processes—treating patients and recording patient care data—thereby increasing the value provided to the customer.

Enabling New Valuable Processes

AT&T's SmartPhone is a good example of enabling new processes:

AT&T recently began selling a new product called the SmartPhone, a new phone which can be used to make calls or access information. The device itself is simple to use yet contains a sophisticated computer with a touch-screen display and built-in communications capabilities. AT&T has also designed network processors that enable phone companies and other service providers . . . to extend services accessible by SmartPhone to their customers.

A caller simply pushes the big numbers displayed on its 4-by-6½-inch screen to dial a number or access a service. The computer can visually present menus with scores of services that the customer selects by merely touching the screen. For example, a banking service allows customers to check account balances, transfer funds among accounts, and automatically pay bills without going to the bank.

---

[2]"Electronic Patient Charts," *PC Week*, February 20, 1989, p. 60.

Through SmartPhone, AT&T is looking to keep its commanding lead in the consumer phone market and maintain its influence over future telephone and network design.[3]

By rethinking business processes for customers, AT&T developed new goods and services that increased the value to their customers.

Successfully Reengineering Processes

Many things are necessary for a successful reengineering effort. Let us mention just a few critical success factors[4]:

1. *Secure executive sponsorship.* Because reengineering results in fundamental changes in business processes, organization structure, the use of IT, and business measurements, executive support is critical. This support should be obtained at the outset. Without it, any efforts to reengineer will likely be thwarted by those resisting change.

2. *Businesspeople should manage reengineering efforts.* Too often, IT and IT professionals lead reengineering efforts. When this occurs, technology begins to be the focus rather than solving business problems. Reengineering is not something IT professionals can do for, or to, an organization. To solve business problems you must involve businesspeople and others who operate the process.

3. *Get everyone in the organization involved.* The message that must be given to the entire organization is that reengineering will affect all processes, people, and systems. Key businesspeople across the organization should be given the opportunity to provide ideas and input for modifying and improving the process. However, an organization's reengineering efforts must not be delayed or postponed by resistance to change. Everyone must be given the opportunity to lead, follow, or get out of the way. For this to be possible, everyone needs to develop an enterprisewide, instead of parochial, perspective.

4. *Survey large fields and cultivate small ones.* Everyone involved should understand the big picture, but focus reengineering efforts on

---

[3] "SmartPhone Has Milestone: First Customer," *The Wall Street Journal*, March 19, 1991, p. B5.

[4] Some of our suggestions are quite similar to those proposed by Don Tapscott and Art Caston in their book *Paradigm Shift*, published by McGraw-Hill, 1992.

smaller, more manageable processes. When the big picture is missing, people tend to become parochial. When efforts are not focused on the manageable, people begin trying to "boil the ocean" so to speak. Proper balance between perspectives and purposes requires the constant attention and involvement of management paying careful attention to the costs and benefits of the overall and individual efforts.

5. *Assess costs and benefits.* Unless the costs and benefits of a proposed change can be clearly identified, and the benefits provide an adequate return on the cost of investment, there is little reason to proceed with change. However, assessing costs and benefits should not focus solely on financially quantifiable aspects of the proposal. Many costs and benefits are not quantifiable in a traditional sense, but are every bit as important to consider. Cost/benefit analysis should provide a set of measurements for assessing the results of changes to determine whether the goals of the project were actually met.

6. *You can't change what you can't measure.* Any efforts to change business processes will require changes in measurements. Sometimes the measurements will include traditional parameters such as cost/profit ratios, reduced cost per unit of output, or increased revenues. However, alternative measures may at times be more effective in assessing the impact of changes in process quality, customer satisfaction, or to rework errors.

7. *Communicate or fail.* Because reengineering typically cuts across functional boundaries, everyone must be kept informed. Surprises generally cause resistance, if not open rebellion.

8. *Keep your eye out for "low hanging fruit."* Not all reengineering efforts are major projects that require convening a session of congress every time you want to make a change. There will frequently be opportunities to simplify processes which require a minimal amount of work. Taking advantage of these opportunities can provide momentum, encouragement, and credibility for reengineering efforts.

Reengineering requires that everyone be involved in critical introspection and be constantly improving the way an organization works. As Michael Hammer emphasizes, we must think using a blank piece of paper. Sometimes this results in fairly minor alterations, but frequently results in major changes. Reengineering requires an organization to constantly analyze its processes to identify what is essential and then initiate movement toward accomplishing it as efficiently and effectively as possible.

As valuable as reengineering is, there are risks inherent in reengineering. Many times those involved in reengineering do not properly assess the risks an organization faces. Reengineering focuses on making processes as efficient and effective as possible. Controls focus on minimizing, or possibly eliminating, process risk. Traditionally, controlling business and information-processing risk has either been addressed grudgingly or wholly ignored. Either approach is dangerous and of little value. There is an alternative.

CONTROLLING BUSINESS AND INFORMATION PROCESS RISK

Today Murphy's Law is alive and well in organizations—that which can go wrong will! While attempting to make processes more efficient and effective, organizations are facing an increasingly risky environment and are becoming much more susceptible to risk. To make matters worse, simply applying IT magnifies the impact of poorly designed business and information processes. For example, during the 1980s several large stock brokerage companies developed sophisticated computerized trading systems to "improve" the trading process. While building these systems, no one would have ever imagined the potential embarrassment which at least one brokerage firm realized. On March 26, 1992, *The Wall Street Journal* reported:

> A Salomon Brothers, Inc. clerk hit the wrong button on a program-trading terminal and sent a huge electronic sell order for as much as $500 million of stock cascading onto the New York Stock Exchange just before the closing bell yesterday. The huge sell order, involving about 50 major stocks, caused virtual chaos on the Big Board floor in the closing minutes of trading, knocking the Dow Jones Industrial Average down by nearly 12 points, turning what had been a modest gain into a 1.57-point loss. "It happened in the last minute; the orders were peppered all over the place," said one stunned Big Board trader. "There was no inkling of it; all of a sudden it came in at 3:58 and 3:59 and it just rolled across the floor, all delivered by computer. This was a misguided missile." In a brief statement last night, Salomon said it "made an error today in executing a customer's order. Salomon expects to correct the error through market transactions over the next few days."[5]

---

[5]W. Power, and C. Torres, "Stocks Drop As Salomon Clerk Errs," *The Wall Street Journal*, March 26, 1992, p. C1.

Unless there is a fundamental change in philosophy regarding risk, controls, and auditing we can expect to see more and more losses from poorly managed risk. The question is, "How do you develop controls while facilitating reengineering efforts?" We suggest four steps:

1. Identify the business and information process risks and assess the significance or materiality of each.

2. Identify the control(s) needed for each significant risk.

3. Develop, test, and implement the control(s).

4. Periodically evaluate and refine the controls.

There are an infinite number of risks an organization can face and the significance of each can vary widely. We will focus on three types of risk: business process risk, information processing risk, and technological risk. These three types of risk can be controlled more effectively and efficiently by changing one's philosophy and more effectively using IT. As we gain control of these three types of risks we can turn our attention more effectively to the other types of risk. Figure 4-1 contains a taxonomy of potential errors associated with these three types of risk.

Business Process Risks

Business process risks are the risks of errors or irregularities in processing individual business events and/or entire business processes. The following are several types of errors and irregularities dealing with a business process. One or more business events:

Occur at the wrong time.

Occur in the wrong sequence.

Involve an unauthorized internal agent.

Involve the wrong external agent.

Involve the wrong resource.

Involve the wrong amount of resource.

Occur at the wrong location.

Do not trigger necessary subsequent business or information processes.

Each of these conditions can result in embarrassment or loss to the organization. When left unaddressed, they may even result in the organization's

FIGURE 4-1
Taxonomy of Risk

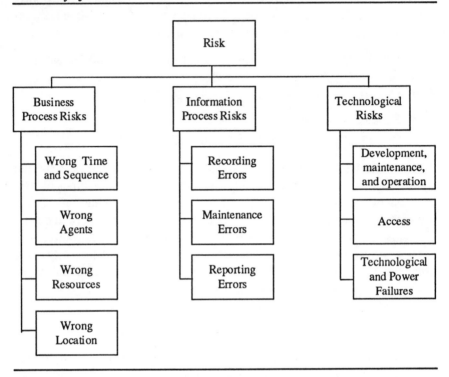

demise. Notice that the same characteristics—resources, events, agents, and locations—used to describe the essential nature of business events also help reveal the types of risks in business processes. Therefore, while capturing business event data, we need to execute controls which can prevent or detect these errors and irregularities in real time so the organization can respond in a timely and effective manner.

Information Processing Risks

Business events trigger three types of information processes: recording business event data; maintaining data about resources, agents, and locations; or reporting information to information customers. The following risks relate to information processing.

Errors and irregularities in recording business event data. Recording errors and irregularities deal with recording incomplete or inaccurate data about a business event. Incomplete data does not contain all the relevant characteristics about the business event. Inaccurate data arises from recorded data being either invalid or improperly valued. Invalid data includes data that is recorded about a fabricated event. Improperly valued data includes inaccurate data recorded about a real event.

Errors and irregularities in maintaining resource, agent, and location data. Maintenance risks are essentially the same as those involved in recording data except they relate to reference information that is not kept current. The risk relating to maintenance processes is that changes with respect to the organization's resources, agents, and locations will go either undetected or unrecorded (e.g., customer moves, customer declares bankruptcy, or a vendor changes telephone numbers). The need for changes in resource, agent, and location data is the result of business events, but they are not necessarily within the span of control of the organization who is trying to maintain the data. Some of the events are among those planned, controlled, and evaluated by the organization itself (e.g., sale, cash receipt, shipping, or assembly). Many events, however, occur outside the control of the organization (e.g., resources become unavailable, an employee gets married or has a child, or a vendor goes out of business). Therefore, maintaining accurate data about resources, agents, and locations is absolutely critical.

Errors and irregularities in reporting business information. Reporting risks include data classification, timing, and valuation. Data classification risk is the risk the data could be improperly classified per some classification criteria (e.g., classifying a fixed asset as cash, classifying an order as a purchase, or classifying a customer as a vendor). Timing risk involves either including or excluding data improperly while generating information. Valuation risk involves the improper conversion of data from one value to another (e.g., improperly converting dollars to yen, guilders to francs, meters to feet, or pounds to kilograms). Additionally, reporting risk includes the risk of providing information to unauthorized information customers or not providing the information in a timely manner.

This discussion does not include improperly classifying business event data as a recording error. As explained earlier, classifying business event data is part of the reporting process. This includes the classification of business events as debits or credits. When we attempt to control classification risk by restricting the way data is recorded (e.g., with debits or credits and account codes), we actually complicate the problem particularly when we recognize, and attempt to respond to, different or conflicting classification schemes. To avoid this problem, we should capture a complete description of business events and their related agents, resources, and locations and then apply classification criteria when extracting data.

Although all information processing errors and irregularities are undesirable whenever they occur, they are particularly harmful when they occur during the recording and maintenance processes. The old adage, "Garbage in, Garbage out!," accurately describes our inability to establish processing controls that can correct for earlier errors in the recording process. If inaccurate or incomplete data is either recorded or maintained, the output of all subsequent reporting processes will be erroneous regardless of the quality of the reporting process or the technology utilized. Furthermore, if the recording process also executes management's policy surrounding a business event and the logic of the recording process is faulty, the recording process can also allow errors and irregularities in the business process itself.

Technological Risk

Our discussion of risk to this point has not taken into consideration the risk associated with technology itself. This is purposeful. When business and information process risk is properly evaluated and controlled, identifying and controlling technological risk is far more straightforward. Controlling technological risk deals with controlling the risk associated with:

1. Developing, maintaining, and operating IT uses.
2. Accessing IT.
3. Failing IT and power.

Volumes have been written regarding the controlling of IT risks, so we will not belabor the point. Our focus has been on assessing and controlling business and information processing risk which often appears to be at odds with reengineering efforts. The two, in fact, are not only compatible, but they complement one another. The achievement of both is not only desirable, but essential. Focusing on business events facilitates the achievement of what has been considered mutually exclusive goals.

RISK AND HUMAN BEHAVIOR

Even though we may become quite successful in controlling all other types of risk, the risk associated with human behavior cannot be overlooked or overemphasized. Little can be done to prevent employees who are determined to embarrass, damage, or destroy an organization except to avoid hiring these people. Therefore, significant emphasis should be placed on hiring honest, trustworthy, and reliable individuals. Controlling risk requires the cooperation of employees. Employees are among the most critical components of control, particularly over business and information process risk. Sound personnel practices are essential. The quality of an organization's employees directly influences both the quality of the goods and services provided by the organization and the quality of controls.

Generally speaking, competent, trustworthy employees are more likely to help the organization create value and control risk. Fostering ethics requires constant attention on the part of management. When properly led, employees can become a critical part of controls over business and information process risk as well as over the general success of the organization in providing value to customers. Otherwise, humans can begin manifesting some dangerously dysfunctional behavior. The epidemic of computer viruses is proof of the danger of dysfunctional human behavior and the need to include employees in controlling risk.

PHILOSOPHICAL ISSUES TO RESOLVE

The concepts we have presented represent a substantial change in philosophy regarding reengineering and controlling risk. We will continue to address reengineering and risk issues throughout the book, but we do not intend to provide an exhaustive catalogue of reengineered business and information processes and their associated risks and controls. To become effective at reengineering and controlling business and information processes requires substantial experience and new thinking.

Auditors have traditionally had responsibility to develop, implement, and evaluate controls. However, auditors alone cannot address the risks organizations face today without working closely with IT professionals and without being involved in reengineering efforts.

Auditors are often excluded from reengineering projects. This exclusion, or limited involvement is costly and potentially dangerous for the organization. Auditors must work with reengineering teams to create business solutions which facilitate continual improvements in controls over business and information process and risk. To help auditors become a valuable part of a reengineering effort, a few points of philosophy need to be discussed.

The Vanishing Audit Trail— Myth or Reality?

Auditors rely on the physical visibility of data to establish what is commonly called the "audit trail." The traditional definition of the audit trail is the collection of documents which allows auditors to trace the processing of accounting numbers back to their source. Some auditors argue that without paper documentation the audit trail is no longer visible or reliable. Organizations may eliminate the use of tangible (paper) documentation, but the ability to trace accounting output to source data can remain intact and become even more visible and reliable than with paper.

For example, in the summer of 1992 Borland International and Symantec, two large computer software companies, became embroiled in a battle over an executive leaving Borland and going to Symantec. Borland accused the executive and Symantec of trade-secret violations. To support their claim, Borland produced a detailed electronic history of mail messages passed between the Borland executive and Symantec which provided details of conversations between the two during the months prior to the move. Such a detailed audit trail would have been nearly impossible with a paper-based system. This is just one example of how IT can be creatively utilized to construct audit trails.

Auditors must realize that the audit trail is only a map consisting of both data and processes which allow auditors to test the integrity of a system's data. In an electronic environment, the audit trail also consists of both data and processes. However, the primary difference is that the electronic audit trail has the potential of being far less complex and much more "visible" than in a paper-based audit trail. Continued reliance on human and paper processes is both inadequate and costly. Holding to such beliefs only makes the transition toward new business processes and more effective control mechanisms more prolonged and painful.

Financial/Nonfinancial Systems Gap

Auditors must also work to close the gap between financial and nonfinancial systems to become more effective in preventing, rather than simply detecting, errors and irregularities in business processes. Because of the gap between financial and nonfinancial systems, accountants exercise limited and primarily detective control over few, if any, business and information processes. The gap is both unnecessary and costly. Closing the gap provides the opportunity for auditors to be much more involved in controlling business and information processing risk, something that is sorely needed in organizations today.

Separation of Duties

Auditors have relied heavily on what is called "separation of duties." The separation of duties concept is the business equivalent of the Constitution's balance of power among executive, legislative, and judicial arms of government. It is used to structure work assignments so the work of one individual checks the work of another. By separating potentially incompatible functions, we either prevent or detect process errors and irregularities performed by employees. In manual information processing environments, the following separation of duties has proven effective:

> Separate the custody of organization resources (e.g., cash, inventory, or finished goods) from record-keeping.

> Separate the authorization to execute business events from the custody of related assets.

> Separate operational responsibility from record-keeping.

The problem today, however, is that the use of IT can directly challenge the traditional division of responsibilities in the interest of making the organization more efficient and effective. Part of the fifth solution concept presented in Chapter Two (business event data are recorded in real time during the execution of the business event by the agents participating in the event) directly challenges the traditional separation of duties concept suggesting that those executing business events are responsible for recording all relevant business event information. In event-driven business solutions the computer fills the role of one or more of the duties traditionally performed by humans. As a result, the controls provided through separation of human involvement can be replaced by automated processes.

The questions is, "Should we be alarmed by not having the traditional separation of duties?" We think not! Separation of duties in a human processing environment cannot monitor everything each employee does to see that the employee is not innocently making mistakes or purposefully doing harm to the organization. Such an approach is infeasible both physically and economically. However, a well-designed solution utilizing modern information technology can provide much of the observation capabilities we lack in manual information systems and provides much more control over processing. Specifically, information technology can be used to:

Facilitate the capturing of reliable business event data.

Ensure the proper execution of management policy.

More effectively detect, and often prevent errors and irregularities.

Provide increased control over organization resources.

Perform independent checks on both the execution of business events and the processing of business data.

The critical issue is in making sure those developing business solutions take into account the risk associated with business- and information-processes in order to develop the needed controls to prevent, detect, and correct errors and irregularities. Unfortunately, most IT professionals have often ignored business and information processing risk unless a persistent auditor happened to notice a particular risk and demanded the system under development include proper controls to mitigate the risk. Such adversarial relations are neither enjoyable or necessary. With a new philosophy, auditors can significantly enhance an organization's system of internal controls while facilitating business and information process reengineering at the same time.

Size of an Organization and Internal Controls

Auditors generally consider it more difficult to establish an effective system of internal controls in small organizations because of their limited resources and the dependence on traditional concepts. However, when IT is properly used, it is very feasible to develop solutions that provide the necessary controls so that even small businesses have the potential to greatly increase their controls over risk without incurring costs which exceed the benefit of controls.

Tolerable Error Versus Error Elimination

Auditing must shift from a tolerable error concept to an error elimination concept. The traditional audit approach has a built in tolerance for error which is in direct conflict with the focus on error elimination in business and information processes. Granted, error elimination may not always be achievable. However, this should be the objective. Manufacturing processes have shown that tolerable errors can become compounded until their cumulative effect is far beyond what is tolerable. The resulting costs of product and lost faith of customers can be substantial.

Built-In Versus Built On Controls

Another key to successfully controlling business risk is having the right philosophy on implementing controls. Simply put, business solutions supporting the organization should have the controls to prevent and detect business event errors and irregularities built right into its recording, maintenance, and reporting processes.

Internal control should not be viewed as something that must be superimposed on an organization's normal operating structure. To do so only means costs that can inhibit the organization's ability to compete. Internal control should be *built into* the infrastructure of an enterprise. When controls are integrated with operational activities, and a focus on controls has been instilled in all personnel, the result is better control with minimum incremental cost. Such integration avoids a superstructure of control procedures on top of existing activities. Whenever management considers changes to their company's operations or activities, the concept that it's better to 'build-in' rather than 'build-on' controls, and to do it right the first time, should be fundamental guiding premises.[6]

Building in controls which are executed as part of business and information processes moves auditing from being an afterthought to making auditing more of a real time activity. Unfortunately, all too many auditors and IT professionals encourage and perpetuate a separation of duties between the two; an unfortunate and costly philosophy.

Taken together, what we are suggesting is no doubt controversial. Nevertheless, these concepts are critical for business solution professionals. Controlling risk is a critical and valuable service to offer, but the way it is done must be improved.

---

[6]*Internal Control: Integrated Framework*, (New York: Committee of Sponsoring Organizations of the Treadway Commission, 1992).

The question to ask now is, "What is the impact of all this on auditor independence?" Auditor independence is certainly important and must not be compromised. Involving auditors in developing business and information processes has the potential to impair their independence. Rules may need to be established that require one set of auditors for evaluating a system and another set for developing the system. Perhaps rules ought to be established that require auditors to be involved during the development process. Auditors have a lot to offer but are currently being either restricted or inhibited from creatively helping facilitate change and control risk.

Auditors cannot expect organizations or society to tolerate the traditional philosophy and its corresponding weaknesses. As John Burton, former chief accountant for the SEC, has observed, as IT developments

> supplant traditional reporting, dramatic changes will necessarily affect public accountants in a substantial way. Traditionally, the public accountant has primarily viewed himself as the auditor of financial statements; under the new system, financial statements will play a dramatically less significant role. The likelihood that substantial fees will continue to be paid for an auditor's assurance that the statements "present fairly according to GAAP" [. . . will be open to questions.] If they see the profession's business as information and communication, their prospects are excellent, since that is where the action will be . . . . On the other hand, if they see themselves as auditors of financial statements, their fruit is likely to wither on the vine.[7]

Our experience suggests that auditors have a tremendous role to play in reengineering business processes and improving controls over risk. We have found that focusing on business events facilitates the simultaneous achievement of continually improving business processes while also improving controls over business and information process risk. This, however, does require a substantial change of philosophy and objective to guide information professionals focusing on developing event-driven business solutions.

---

[7]J.C. Burton, "Dean Burton Urges Accountants to Embrace New Technologies," *The Week in Review*, Deloitte Haskins & Sells, October 26, 1984, pp. 1–3.

Chapter Five

Defining Event-Driven Business Solution Requirements
How to Identify and Integrate Data and Processes.

THE BIG PICTURE

We now come to the point where the rubber meets the road. Throughout the first four chapters we described the underlying concepts of event-driven business solutions and discussed their impact on, and relationship to, a variety of issues. Now it is time to turn our attention to implementing the concepts.

Although we intend to be thorough in our explanation, we will keep our explanation at a fairly high level. Instead of providing an exhaustive tutorial we will illustrate the nature of event-driven business solution requirements and the basic definition process. Becoming proficient in this process requires more time and experience than can be gained by simply reading a chapter of a book. Developing an expertise in defining event-driven solution requirements requires hands-on training and practical application.[1]

Let's start by putting this chapter in context. The process of creating any deliverable has four phases as illustrated in Figure 5–1:

✓ Define deliverable requirements.
✓ Develop the deliverable.

---

[1]Those interested in detailed training should contact the authors directly to obtain more information about training we offer.

FIGURE 5-1
The Traditional Development Process

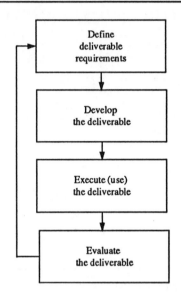

✓ Execute (use) the deliverable.

✓ Evaluate the deliverable.

This process has been used to create all kinds of deliverables ranging from cars to houses to roads to government programs to computers to computerized systems. The idea is to visualize the end result before expending the resources to actually develop and use the deliverable. Once the deliverable is in use, evaluation typically leads to the definition of new requirements and the process starts over again. Ideally, the creation process never should stop.

Although this process is well known and increases the likelihood of success, it has some significant weaknesses. When the process is applied to developing business solutions, these weaknesses can result in tremendous inefficiencies and can threaten the likelihood of success. From a businessperson's perspective, the process has the following weakness (see Figure 5–2):

Too slow. Plain and simple, traditional efforts to define, develop, and install a solution take too long. Given the dynamic environment facing

FIGURE 5-2
Weaknesses of the Traditional Development Process

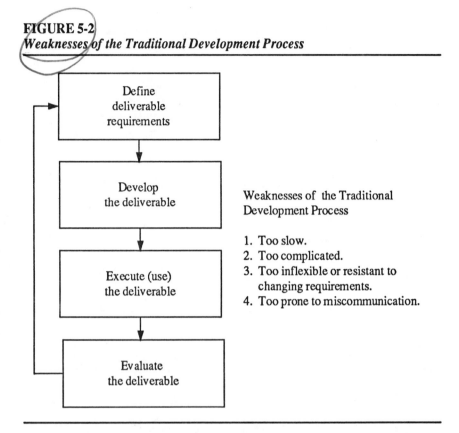

Weaknesses of the Traditional
Development Process

1. Too slow.
2. Too complicated.
3. Too inflexible or resistant to changing requirements.
4. Too prone to miscommunication.

organizations today, the traditional development process is both inadequate and dangerous. Organizations can't wait for the development of solutions that are out of date before they are used.

Too complicated. The process is much too complicated for both businesspeople and solution developers. The variety of tasks, techniques, and tools utilized in traditional systems development methodologies require a heavy, up-front investment to be able to participate in even the initial efforts to define solution requirements. Furthermore, from a businessperson's perspective, the traditional process focuses more on IT than on business problems.

Too inflexible or resistant to changing requirements. Solution developers often try to get businesspeople to say once and for all "this is what

I want." The reason for this effort is to prevent having someone introduce new requirements later in the development process that result in the need to modify work on an earlier phase. Redoing earlier work is costly and threatens the viability of a project. The fact is, getting businesspeople to clearly state their requirements once and for all is both unlikely and undesirable. Misperceived or overlooked requirements make this almost impossible. We must accept the fact that requirements can, will, and should change. The solution development process must be able to adapt to this reality.

Too prone to miscommunication (see Figure 5–3). Miscommunication can cripple or even destroy a project. When miscommunication occurs, particularly in communicating solution requirements, it does not matter how much we have overcome the other weaknesses, the development project will not be successful.

Individually, each of these weaknesses is significant. Collectively, they make the process too ineffective and inefficient. The costs, coupled with the other weaknesses, often result in guarded involvement, interest, and support

FIGURE 5-3
Miscommunication in the Traditional Development Process

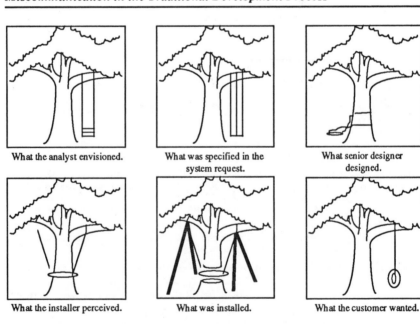

| What the analyst envisioned. | What was specified in the system request. | What senior designer designed. |

| What the installer perceived. | What was installed. | What the customer wanted. |

on the part of businesspeople. Furthermore, the magnitude of these weaknesses increases as the size, importance, and complexity of the desired solution increases.

The question is, How do we address the fundamental weaknesses of the development process? We have found that many of these weaknesses can be addressed by applying the event-driven concepts while defining requirements. The remainder of this chapter describes the event-driven approach to defining solution requirements.

 ## DEFINING BUSINESS SOLUTION REQUIREMENTS

Underneath all the high tech glitz and glitter, solution requirements have four parts (see Figure 5-4). The solution:

✓ Context or scope.

✓ Data.

✓ Processes.

✓ Interfaces.

FIGURE 5-4   ✓
Event-Driven Solution Components

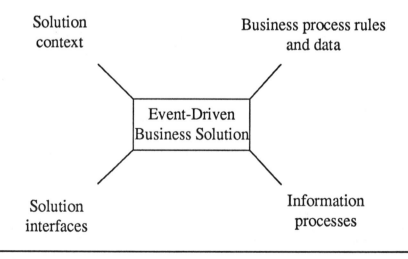

Each part defines a specific aspect of the solution requirements. Collectively, they form a cohesive definition of the essence of the solution requirements that can be validated and implemented. Our discussion of defining solution requirements focuses on defining a solution's context, data, and processes. A great deal has already been written regarding interface design. Event-driven solution concepts fit nicely with current interface design principles.[2]

Modeling and prototyping techniques facilitate the identification of essential solution requirements. Four simple techniques are sufficient (see Figure 5–5):

FIGURE 5-5
Event-Driven Solution Component Definition Techniques

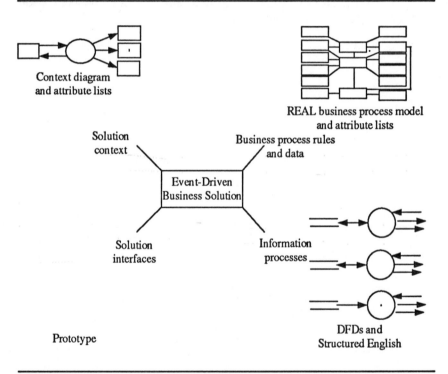

Context diagram
and attribute lists

REAL business process model
and attribute lists

Solution
context

Business process rules
and data

Event-Driven
Business Solution

Solution
interfaces

Information
processes

Prototype

DFDs and
Structured English

---

[2]One of the more concise guides to interface principles and design is IBM's *Common User Access Advanced Interface Design Guide* (SC26-4582-0), 1989. This publication can be acquired through any IBM representative.

Modeling the solution context.

Modeling business process rules and data.

Modeling information processes.

Prototyping.

Those familiar with traditional systems analysis techniques will likely recognize the tools utilized to illustrate our techniques. However, the solution process is not dependent upon a specific type of tool. In fact we have used a variety of tools with equal success. The choice of tools should be driven by what communicates best with businesspeople. What is important are the techniques guiding how the tools are used and integrated. Therefore, the techniques we will explain can be applied to any preferred modeling tool.

The process of defining event-driven solution requirements involves four *Four* concurrent tasks illustrated in Figure 5–6: *Tasks*

FIGURE 5-6
The Event-Driven Solution Definition Process

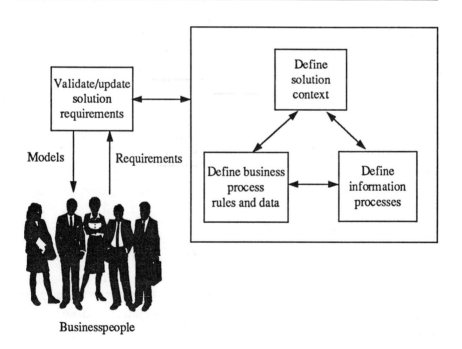

Define the solution context.

Define the business process rules and data.

Define the information processes.

Validate/update solution requirements.

Although these are concurrent processes, we will not attempt to present them concurrently. Instead, we will discuss each task and then discuss how they interrelate and are developed concurrently.

Define the Scope

DEFINE BUSINESS SOLUTION CONTEXT

Why is a solution context important? Defining the context serves to coordinate the perceptions of everyone involved in defining solution requirements. Without a fairly clear definition of a solution scope we run the risk of trying to "boil the ocean," so to speak. As a result, the solution definition process quickly becomes unachievable and resembles a prank final exam that asks students to model the universe and give three examples. However, with a clear definition of scope, subsequent work is focused and the chance of misperception is reduced.

The solution context describes the underlying business events/processes, solution inputs and outputs, and sources and destinations of inputs and outputs. Let's take a look at each aspect of the solution context.

Underlying business events and processes. The context of an event-driven business solution is defined by the business events and processes within its scope. Therefore, the context can range from a single business event (e.g., sale, cash receipt, or purchase) to a complete business processes (e.g., the acquisition/payment process, the conversion process, or the sales/collection process). As we noted in Chapter Three, the nature of business processes vary by type of resource, agent, or location involved. Therefore, to scope the definition effort, solution contexts typically focus on a subset of a general process (e.g., the sale event of a sales/collection process) or on a special version of the process for a specific resource, agent, or location (e.g., sales/collection process for general merchandise versus sales/collection process for services).

Solution inputs and outputs. The solution context includes characteristics of solution inputs (data) and outputs (information). Without descriptions of data and information flows, there is little to guide the definition of solution details.

Sources and destinations of inputs and outputs. Inputs to a solution originate from a variety of sources and outputs and are delivered to a variety of destinations. Sources and destinations can include people, organizations, automated devices, and interfaces with other systems which do not subscribe to the event-driven solution concepts.

Although all the aspects of the solution context must eventually be defined, specifics regarding various aspects of a context can be added incrementally while defining solution data and processes. This allows the context to take shape as businesspeople and solution professionals become more acquainted with the solution requirements rather than attempting to identify and freeze the definition of every characteristic of the solution context from the outset.

Details of a solution context can be documented using a simple diagram (see Figure 5–7). Those familiar with traditional modeling tools will recognize the diagram as a 0 level data flow diagram. Three symbols are used to represent various aspects of a solution context:

The *circle* represents the underlying business process—in the example, the underlying business process is the sales/collection process.

Arrows represent solution inputs and outputs—in the example, the arrow labeled Order represents an input while the arrows labeled Order Confirmation, Marketing Info, and Accounting Info each represent outputs.

Squares represent input sources and output destinations—in the example, the box labeled Customer represents both an input source and an output destination while the boxes labeled Marketing Management and Investors/Creditors represent output destinations.

Notice that details regarding the solution inputs and outputs are included. Input/output details are referred to collectively as the context dictionary. Context dictionary notation is fairly straightforward. Each label in the diagram becomes the name of an entry in the context dictionary. Each definition begins with an equal sign (=) to the right of the entry name. The

FIGURE 5-7
Diagram of Solution Definition Process

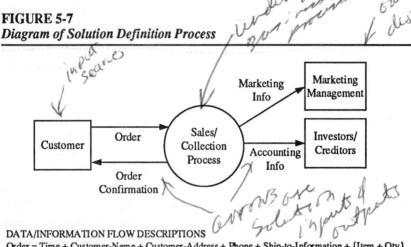

DATA/INFORMATION FLOW DESCRIPTIONS

Order = Time + Customer-Name + Customer-Address + Phone + Ship-to-Information + {Item + Qty}
Order-Confirmation = Confirmation# + Customer-Name + Customer-Address + Phone + {Item# + Item-
    Description + Qty-Ordered + Order-Price} + Ship-to-Info + Subtotal + Tax +
    Total-Order-Amount
Marketing-Info = (Product-Margin-Report, Product-Catalogue, Salesperson-Performance-Report)
Product-Margin-Report = Report-Date + {Item# + Units-Sold + $Volume + Unit-Margin }+
    Total-Units-Sold + Total-$Volume + Avg-Unit-Margin
Salesperson-Performance-Report = Report-Date + {Salesperson-ID + Name + Commission-Rate +
    Units-Sold + $Volume + Avg-Unit-Margin}
Product-Catalogue = Item# + Description + Color + Size + Current-Price + Current-Cost
Accounting-Info = Revenue + Cost-of-Goods-Sold + Gross-Margin + Accounts-Receivable

detailed elements of the input or output are then listed to the right of the equal sign and are separated by plus signs (+). Elements which repeat within a definition are enclosed in brackets ({}). For example, the entry Order is defined as the combination of the Time of the order, the Customer-Name, Customer-Address, Phone, and Ship-to-Information. Enclosing Item and Qty in the {} symbols means several items and their respective quantities can be specified within a single order.

Context definitions can be nested in the context dictionary as well. To simplify the context diagram only one input flow and one output flow is identified graphically for each source and destination. If a source or destination has more than one inflow or outflow, the one flow is given a general label and the labels of each flow are nested in the data/information flow definitions. For example, the output flow Marketing-Info includes three output flows (Product-Margin-Report, Product-Catalogue, and Salesperson-Performance-Report). The definitions of each specific flow can then be provided as separate entries in the context dictionary.

After an initial discussion regarding the solution's context, the remaining time spent on defining solution requirements is a parallel effort focusing on defining the context, data, and processes of the solution. Throughout the data and process definition work, however, we can continue to make modifications to the solution context diagram to reflect an increased understanding of the solution context.

DEFINE SOLUTION DATA

The REAL business process models introduced in Chapter Three are the basis for defining business process rules and data (see Figure 5–8). These models provide an efficient and effective means of defining and organizing solution data. What is needed is the addition of some details regarding the resources, events, agents, and locations in the model and their relationships. To do so we need to introduce a few new concepts and tools.

FIGURE 5-8
REAL Business Process Model of Mail Order Sales/Collection Process

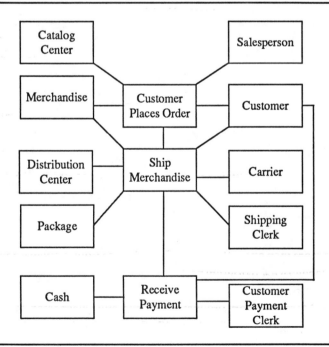

Entities and Occurrences

Entities, for our purposes, are conceptual objects which collectively describe business processes. REAL business process models have four entity types: resources, events, agents, and locations. Entity occurrences are specific examples of each entity type. For example, for the resource entity Merchandise, specific occurrences might be Item # 1, Item # 2, Item # 3, etc. Specific occurrences of the event entity Sale might include Sale # 1, Sale # 2, Sale # 3, etc. Furthermore, specific occurrences of the agent entity Salesperson might include Salesperson # 1, Salesperson # 2, Salesperson # 3, etc.

Relationship Cardinalities

A relationship cardinality describes how occurrences of two entities are related (Figure 5–9). Including relationship cardinalities provides greater details about the business rules associated with a business process. Furthermore, once the underlying resources, events, agents, and locations are identified we can describe a variety of business rules by simply changing the

FIGURE 5-9
Entity Occurrences and Relationship Cardinalities

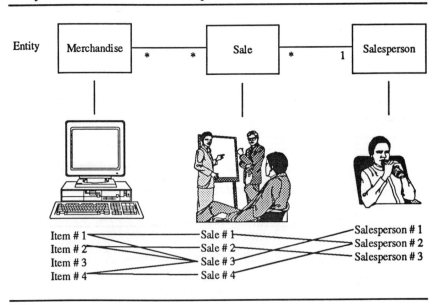

relationship cardinalities. Let's use, as an example, the relationship between two event entities—Purchase and Cash Disbursement.

In Figure 5–10 a one-to-one (1:1) relationship exists between the event entities Purchase and Cash Disbursement. This relationship cardinality describes the business rule *Each Purchase is related to only one Cash Disbursement and each Cash Disbursement is related to only one Purchase*. In the common vernacular, the 1:1 relationships between Purchase and Cash Disbursement describes a cash basis purchase. The 1:1 notation is simply a more efficient and precise means of describing a business rule. However, by changing the nature of the relationship cardinality a completely different situation can be represented.

FIGURE 5-10
1:1 Relationship between Purchase and Cash Disbursement

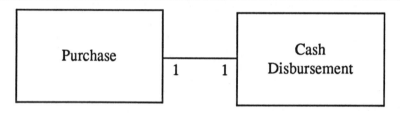

Cash basis purchase

In Figure 5–11 a one-to-many (1:*) relationship exists between Purchase and Cash Disbursement. The 1:* relationship means each Purchase can be related to more than one Cash Disbursement. This describes a typical coupon credit situation when buying large ticket items such as automobiles or buildings. One purchase is associated with many cash disbursements. Reversing the direction of the relationship to many-to-one (*:1), however, describes a completely different situation. In this case a single Cash Disbursement can be related to many Purchases involving credit accounts, for example, when payment is due at the end of each month.

In Figure 5–12 a many to many (*:*) relationship describes yet another business rule using the same entities. This relationship means that each

FIGURE 5-11
1: Relationship between Purchase and Cash Disbursement*

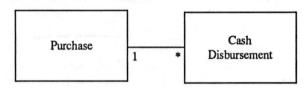

Coupon credit purchase
(e.g., big ticket purchases on credit - car, building, and equipment)

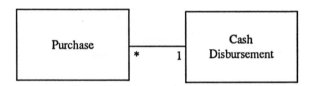

Credit purchases with one payment
(e.g., open account due at end of month)

FIGURE 5-12
: Relationship between Purchase and Cash Disbursement

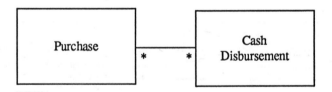

Revolving credit
(e.g., credit card accounts with minimum payments)

Purchase can be related to more than one Cash Disbursement and that each Cash Disbursement can be related to more than one Purchase—a typical revolving credit situation.

As you can see, cardinalities provide a simple, yet powerful means of describing essential rules governing a business process. When cardinality information is included, the REAL business process model (see Figure 5–13) provides an even more detailed representation of the business process. Furthermore, it provides a straightforward means of organizing business data.

FIGURE 5-13
REAL Business Process Model with Cardinalities

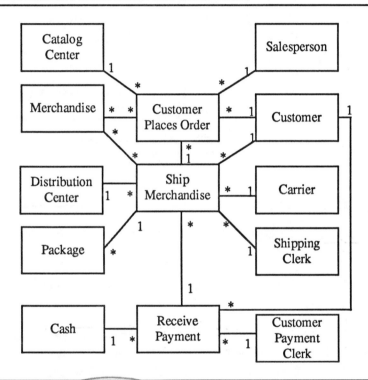

Entity and Relationship Attributes

Entity and relationship attributes provide details regarding a model's resources, events, agents, and locations and their relationships. Defining entity and relationship attributes is guided by both the REAL business process model and the solution context dictionary. The result of each of the following steps is illustrated in Figure 5–14.

FIGURE 5-14
Attribute Lists and the REAL Business Process Model

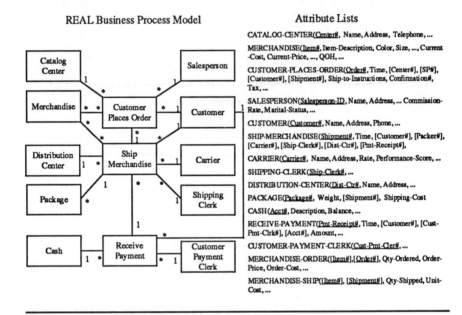

REAL Business Process Model   Attribute Lists

CATALOG-CENTER(Center#, Name, Address, Telephone, ...

MERCHANDISE(Item#, Item-Description, Color, Size, ..., Current -Cost, Current-Price, ..., QOH, ...

CUSTOMER-PLACES-ORDER(Order#, Time, [Center#], [SP#], [Customer#], [Shipment#], Ship-to-Instructions, Confirmation#, Tax, ...

SALESPERSON(Salesperson-ID, Name, Address, ... Commission-Rate, Marital-Status, ...

CUSTOMER(Customer#, Name, Address, Phone, ...

SHIP-MERCHANDISE(Shipment#, Time, [Customer#], [Packer#], [Carrier#], [Ship-Clerk#], [Dist-Ctr#], [Pmt-Receipt#],

CARRIER(Carrier#, Name, Address, Rate, Performance-Score, ...

SHIPPING-CLERK(Ship-Clerk#, ...

DISTRIBUTION-CENTER(Dist-Ctr#, Name, Address, ...

PACKAGE(Package#, Weight, [Shipment#], Shipping-Cost

CASH(Acct#, Description, Balance, ...

RECEIVE-PAYMENT(Pmt-Receipt#, Time, [Customer#], [Cust-Pmt-Clrk#], [Acct#], Amount, ...

CUSTOMER-PAYMENT-CLERK(Cust-Pmt-Clrk#, ...

MERCHANDISE-ORDER([Item#],[Order#], Qty-Ordered, Order-Price, Order-Cost, ...

MERCHANDISE-SHIP([Item#], [Shipment#], Qty-Shipped, Unit-Cost, ...

Step 1. Create an attribute list for each entity in the REAL business process model. For example, in Figure 5–14 the attribute list CATALOG-CENTER is created for the entity Catalog-Center, SALESPERSON for Salesperson, CUSTOMER- PLACES-ORDER for Customer-Places-Order, and so forth.

Step 2. Identify the key attribute(s) for each table. A key attribute is one that can uniquely identify each occurrence of a list. We often create artifacts to uniquely identify occurrences of entities. For example, Customer # is used to uniquely identify occurrences of the CUSTOMER list, Order # for the CUSTOMER-PLACES-ORDER list, or Salesperson ID for the SALES-PERSON list. Key attributes are distinguished in the attribute list by being underlined.

Step 3. Establish relationships among attribute lists per the REAL business process model. The relationship cardinality determines the technique used to establish the relationship. The two most common relationships are 1:* (or *:1) and *:*. The 1:* relationship is represented by placing the key attribute of the entity on the 1 side of a relationship in the attribute table of the entity on the * side of the relationship. For example, the key attribute of CUSTOMER (Customer#) is placed in the CUSTOMER-PLACES-ORDER list to represent the 1:* relationship between the two entities. We call these linking attributes "foreign keys" and use brackets ([]) to differentiate them from other attributes.

Unlike 1:* relationships, *:* relationships are represented by creating a new list to represent the relationship between the two related entities.[3] For example, the *:* relationship between SHIP-MERCHANDISE and MERCHANDISE is represented by the attribute list MERCHANDISE-SHIP. The key attribute of this new list is the combination of the keys of the two entities being related (Item # and Shipment #). The combination of Item # and Shipment # uniquely identifies each occurrence of the MERCHANDISE-SHIP list.

In REAL business process models most *:* relationships occur between event and resource entities. *:* relationships between events and resources require the inclusion of additional attributes to complete the description of the relationship. These attributes describe the quantity and value of the resource for historical purposes. For example, the MERCHANDISE-SHIP list includes the attributes Qty-Shipped and Unit-Cost of the merchandise shipped. Similar quantity and economic measures of the resources involved in the event are included in the MERCHANDISE-ORDER and MATERIAL-SHIP lists. These nonkey attributes complete the description of the relationship between events and resources.

Step 4. Add nonkey attributes to complete the description of the entities. Nonkey attributes are either essential or discretionary. Essential attributes include those that are critical to describing the essence of an entity. Without getting lost in epistemological theory, the following summarizes essential attributes that describe each type of entity:

Events—Time.

Resources—Description, Current-Cost and/or Price.

Agents—Name and communication addresses (e.g., Address, Telephone, or EMail address).

Locations—geopolitical or geographical coordinates.

---

[3]Our reason for not using foreign attributes to represent *:* relationships is primarily for simplicity purposes. We wish to keep all the lists two dimensional. Using foreign keys to describe *:* relationships would result in three-dimensional lists and would unnecessarily complicate the validation and prototyping process.

Discretionary attributes vary widely depending on information customer requirements. Identifying discretionary attributes is guided by the solution context dictionary (see Figure 5–7). For example, in Figure 5–14 Color and Size are included in the MERCHANDISE list because the Product-List description in the solution context dictionary includes the color and size of each item.

Derivable attributes are those specified in the solution context dictionary that can be derived from essential and discretionary data. For example, Total-Units-Sold in the Product-Margin-Report is a derivable attribute. It can be derived by summing the Qty-Ordered attribute of the MERCHANDISE-ORDER list for the specified reporting period.

Typically, you should not include derivable attributes in REAL business process attribute lists. The assumption underlying the exclusion of derivable data is that when all the underlying data is integrated, information customers can generate any derivable information directly from the essential and discretionary attributes whenever needed.

There is little reason to include Total-Units-Sold in the attribute lists because it is redundant and creates reconciliation problems. For example, including Total-Units-Sold in the attribute lists might require periodic reconciliation with the underlying data from which it is derived. An entirely unnecessary operation when Total-Units-Sold can be derived from the essential and discretionary attributes included in the attribute lists. Other examples of derivable attributes in Figure 5–7 include Total-Order-Amount, Unit-Margin, Total-Units-Sold, and Accounts-Receivable-Balance. Traditionally, systems would be developed to reprocess the underlying essential and discretionary data for each type of derivable information, a costly, and unnecessary, approach.

Including derivable data is sometimes necessary when all the events related to a specific resource, agent, or location are not integrated within the event-driven solution architecture. For example, we may need to include a Quantity-on-Hand attribute in the MERCHANDISE attribute list because data about both shipping and receiving of merchandise are not integrated. If data about both shipping and receiving merchandise were integrated, however, Quantity-on-Hand could be derived by taking the difference between merchandise received and merchandise shipped.

As you can see, the attribute lists resulting from the REAL business process model provide a fairly straightforward means of identifying and organizing solution data. The process of creating the lists can involve a variety of people but does not require any overly technical IT skills. Furthermore, these lists represent a direct challenge to the traditional systems architecture resulting in multiple systems to support diverse reporting requirements. The attribute lists describe the details of a single collection of business data that can be used to derive traditionally competing views across the organization.

Not only is the REAL business process model useful for organizing business data, it can be extended to include a variety of other useful information about the business process. A few of the more useful additions include:

Entity Volumes and Frequencies

Volume and frequency measures are helpful in understanding the characteristics of a business process. Volume and frequency measures help identify needed organization structure, business process performance measures, and potential process bottlenecks. They are also useful for planning a business process and specifying management policy surrounding the process. Volume and frequency data can easily be included in parentheses below each entity name (see Figure 5–15).

Additional Relationships Among Entities

Two additional relationship types may be included to describe relationships between agents and resources and between internal agents and external agents. The REAL business process model provides a foundation upon which such relationships can be specified. For example, management may choose to know the relationship between Supplier and Goods/Services (see Figure 5–16). By adding attributes such as Current-Price, Terms-and-Conditions, and QOH to the attribute list representing the relationship, you have the data needed to represent a catalogue of goods and services with potential suppliers and the terms and conditions of each.

Agents can also be related to one another as in the case of assigning a Salesperson to specific Customers (Figure 5–17). In this case management is interested in making sure all customers have a contact with the company and can track the performance of each salesperson with respect to their assigned customers.

FIGURE 5-15
REAL Business Process Model with Volume/Frequency Data

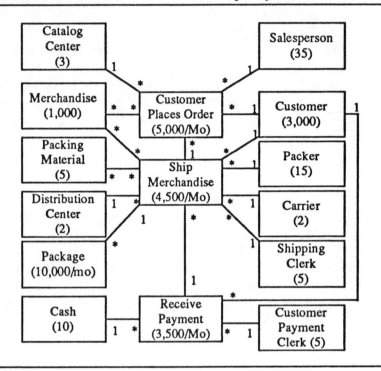

FIGURE 5-16
REAL Business Process Model with Resource/Agent Relationship

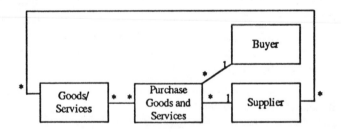

GOOD/SERVICES-SUPPLIER([Item #], [Supplier #], Current-Price, QOH, Terms-and-Conditions, ...

FIGURE 5-17
REAL Business Process Model with External/Internal Agent Relationship

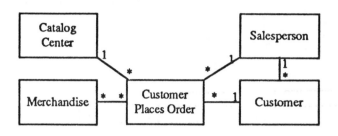

CUSTOMER(Customer #, Name, ... , [Salesperson #], ...

Recursive Relationships

Recursive relationships are useful for relating an occurrence of an entity with another occurrence of the same type of entity (see Figure 5–18). Recursive relationships show how one occurrence can be part of another occurrence. For example, one piece of merchandise is a part of another piece of merchandise (e.g., a watchband is a part of a watch, a steering wheel is part of a car, or a hard disk is part of an assembled computer). The same concept can be applied to agent/agent, event/event, and location/location relationships as well.

Those familiar with traditional data modeling methodologies will notice several unique characteristics of the REAL business process modeling technique. Three of the more significant differences include:

The focus on modeling business processes. Traditional data modeling focuses on decomposing information views and artifacts into conceptual primitives and relationships whereas REAL business process modeling focuses on the underlying business process. Inherent in the REAL modeling technique is a proof that the various information customer views included in the solution context diagram are actually derivable. We will soon see how this difference in focus allows the REAL business process model to be much more adaptive to changing solution requirements.

The focus on enhancing the speed of developing and evaluating the model. The REAL concept provides a template that guides the identifi-

FIGURE 5-18
Example Model of Recursive Relationships and Attribute Tables

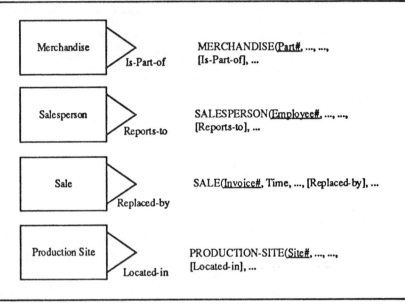

cation of business process entities which can significantly increase the speed of the modeling effort. Furthermore, the template itself provides the basis for validating the model as an accurate representation of the business process.

The focus on communicating with businesspeople. Unlike traditional data models which are often difficult for technical people to understand and validate, REAL business process modeling is fairly straightforward and can be easily understood by nontechnical people. The REAL business process model also provides a useful basis for analyzing other issues relating to organization structure, resource requirements, and process reengineering.

Having identified the business data, the next issue is to define how data and information get in and out of the attribute lists.

DEFINE INFORMATION PROCESSES

In Chapter Three we distinguished business events from information processes. Thus far, we have focused primarily on modeling business events and business processes. Now we need to turn our attention to information processes.

Information processes have the following characteristics:

Inputs.

Process.

Outputs.

Data Stores.

Processing logic.

Two fairly simple tools can be used to represent information process requirements: data flow diagrams (DFDs) and Structured English. DFDs use some of the same conventions we used earlier to model a solution context (see Figure 5-19) and thereby provide a picture of the general characteristics of each individual information process (inputs, outputs, and data). The primary difference between modeling a solution's context and its individual information processes is that DFDs specify data stores but do not include sources and destinations of data and information. We will explain how the two are related in a moment.

FIGURE 5-19
Generic Data Flow Diagram (DFD)

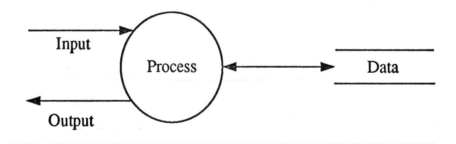

Organizing data around business events greatly simplifies the task of defining information processing requirements. Information processes are needed to perform three basic functions:

Record business event data.

Maintain reference data.

Reporting useful information.

Recording business event data involves capturing data about the business event (e.g., time, participants, location, and resources involved). The recording process executes the business rules specified by management with respect to each business event. Ideally, the execution of the business event and the related information process occurs simultaneously. This allows any critical controls to be executed in real time while also facilitating the real time collection of business data.

Maintaining reference data involves adding, deleting, or modifying data about resources, agents, and locations. Maintenance processes are triggered by the need to know the impact of events occurring outside the scope of an organization's event-driven business solutions. For example, when a supplier creates a new product, discontinues an existing product, or changes the price of a product, we must add, delete, or modify product data unless we have integrated our business data with the supplier. Solution boundaries are becoming blurred as organizations share data about resources, agents, and locations. These kinds of relationships lie at the heart of the notion of extended enterprises who have common resources, agents, and locations across both internal and external organization boundaries.

Reporting focuses on generating outputs (sometimes called views). Outputs are generated to confirm the result of a recording or maintenance process, to respond to a request for information, or to notify someone that an event has occurred. Extracting data from the attribute lists and performing a variety of processes to summarize and format the data are the primary reporting processes.

The three basic information processes are represented graphically using DFDs (see Figure 5–20). Notice that each process has some common characteristics. First, each process is triggered by the receipt of a stimulus. Second, each process interacts with data stores. Third, each process generates both a response and a notification.

Details within each process have a fairly predictable nature. First, stimulus data are edited to insure their integrity. Second, data are stored in appropriate attribute lists. Third, responses and notifications are generated per information customer requirements.

Structured English[4] is used to define the detailed logic of each information process (Figure 5–21). Unlike typical narrative descriptions, Structured

---

[4]The following description of Structured English is adapted from T. DeMarco, *Structured Analysis and System Specification*, (New York: Prentice Hall, 1978).

FIGURE 5-20
Generic Event-Driven Information Processes

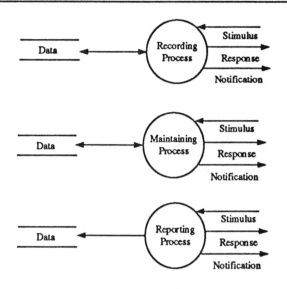

English is a stripped-down version of English which focuses on conciseness and clarity to document the essence of an information process. Structured English eliminates:

Adjectives.

Adverbs.

Compound sentences.

Nonimperative expressions.

All but a limited set of conditional and logic structures.

Most punctuation.

Footnote type details.

So what is left? Structured English! Simply put, Structured English is a language that has a limited vocabulary and syntax. The vocabulary consists of:

Imperative English language verbs.

Terms defined in the context dictionary and attribute lists.

Reserved words used for logic formulation.

FIGURE 5-21
Example of Structured English

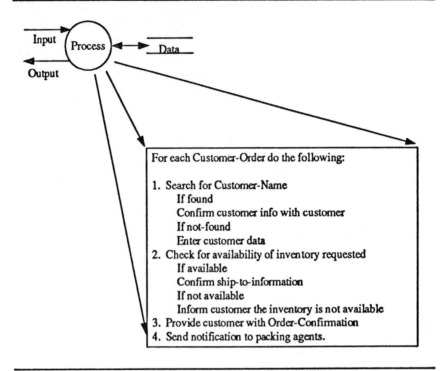

The syntax of Structured English is restricted to three basic logic structures: sequence, choice, and repetition. By combining these three logical building blocks we can describe the details of any solution process and rules.

Although certain aspects of information processes are general, they are not the same. Each organization customizes the nature of the inputs, outputs, and processing logic of the recording, maintaining, and reporting processes. However, when all the unnecessary processing is stripped away, we are left with some simple and predictable processes.

One last note regarding information processes. Recording and maintaining processes are frequently combined. For example, you may want to add a new customer while recording an order, generate a confirmation for the customer, and notify shipping personnel all at the same time. Once the basic components have been defined they can be combined in a variety of ways to satisfy the wide variety of management requirements across business processes and organizations. The basic processing components serve as building blocks for creating business process solutions.

VALIDATE SOLUTION REQUIREMENTS

Solution validation occurs throughout the definition process. In fact, because requirements are constantly changing, validation, like the rest of the definition process, is never really done. The nature and relationship of solution components make the validation process fairly straightforward and efficient. There are two perspectives for validating solution requirements: external validation and internal validation.

External Validation

External validation focuses on the consistency of the model with the real world and the requirements specified by businesspeople. The focus of this evaluation is on the consistency between the model, the actual business processes, and information customer requirements. Three changes can occur during external validation:

First, context inputs and outputs may be added, eliminated, or modified. For example, a new output may be requested by Purchasing Management. This results in the addition of the destination Purchasing Management in the solution context diagram as well as the inclusion of an output (e.g., Inventory-Analysis-Report) and its detailed description as shown in Figure 5–22.

Second, the nature of the underlying business process may change. When the nature of the underlying business process changes, the REAL business process model must be modified to reflect the changes. Changes result in adding, deleting, or modifying process model entities, attributes, or relationships. Figure 5–23 illustrates the impact of management adding inspection and packing events to the mail order sales/collection process as well as the inspector agent role. Furthermore, new attribute lists must be created for the Inspect-Merchandise, Pack-Merchandise, and Inspector entities.

FIGURE 5-22
Modified Solution Context Diagram Reflecting Purchasing Requirements

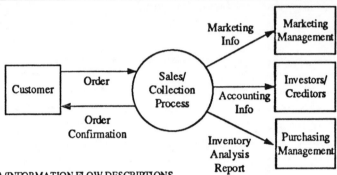

DATA/INFORMATION FLOW DESCRIPTIONS

Order = Time + Customer-Name + Customer-Address + Phone + Ship-to-Information + {Item + Qty}
Order-Confirmation = Confirmation# + Customer-Name + Customer-Address + Phone + {Item# + Item-
    Description + Qty-Ordered + Order-Price} + Ship-to-Info + Subtotal + Tax +
    Total-Order-Amount
Marketing-Info = (Product-Margin-Report, Product-Catalogue, Salesperson-Performance-Report)
Product-Margin-Report = Report-Date + {Item# + Units-Sold + $Volume + Unit-Margin }+
    Total-Units-Sold + Total-$Volume + Avg-Unit-Margin
Salesperson-Performance-Report = Report-Date + {Salesperson-ID + Name + Commission-Rate +
    Units-Sold + $Volume + Avg-Unit-Margin}
Product-Catalogue = Item# + Description + Color + Size + Current-Price + Current-Cost
Accounting-Info = Revenue + Cost-of-Goods-Sold + Gross-Margin + Accounts-Receivable
Inventory-Analysis-Report = Report-Date + {Item# + Units-Sold + Units-On-Hand + Units-on-Order}

Third, the notification destinations on the information processes may change depending on who needs to know about the occurrence of each information process. For example, Treasury may want to know when each order occurs to be able to project cash flows for the future. This information is simply added to the Structured English of the recording process logic.

Again, external validation is an ongoing process resulting in the continual revision of solution requirements.

Internal Validation

When changes are made in the models while assessing the models' external validity, additional changes must be made to maintain the internal validity of the solution models. There are a variety of points among the solution

FIGURE 5-23
Expanded Business Process Model

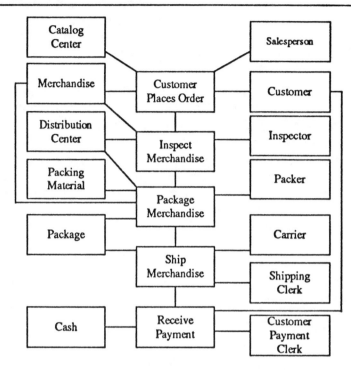

components for assessing the solution's internal validity. Among the most important are the following:

First, information flow details must be included in, or derivable from, the attribute lists associated with the REAL business process model. When solution context requirements change (e.g., a new report for Purchasing Management), the change must be reflected in the attribute lists associated with the REAL business process model. Furthermore, we need to make sure the information required can be read, or derived, from the essential and discretionary attributes included in the REAL business process model attribute tables.

Second, each input and output identified in the solution context diagram must be associated with only one information process model. Specifically, each solution context inflow must correspond to a recording or maintaining process and each outflow must correspond to a reporting process.

Third, each event entity included in the REAL business process model must correspond to an information process. Furthermore, any resource, agent, or location entity must have a corresponding maintenance information process. Therefore, in the earlier example in which the Inspect-Merchandise and Pack-Merchandise events were added, recording information processes must be added. Furthermore, a maintenance process would be needed for the Inspector entity that was added to the REAL business process model.

The internal validation points of event-driven solution requirements are summarized in Figure 5–24.

FIGURE 5-24
Validation Perspectives

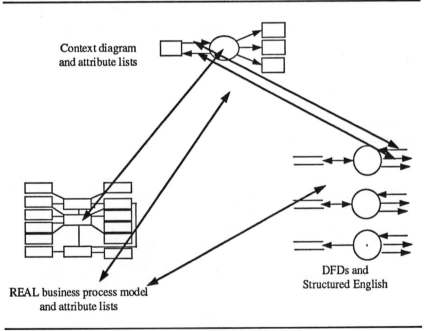

Context diagram and attribute lists

REAL business process model and attribute lists

DFDs and Structured English

Although the models we have presented are quite straightforward and provide a fairly uncomplicated means of validation, there is only so much you can do with static models. We have found that much more dynamic modeling methods are needed to reliably perform the needed external and internal validation. Building a prototype of the requirements fulfills this need.

Translating solution requirements into a prototype is a fairly straightforward process. Microcomputer relational database management systems (e.g., Paradox, FoxPro, or DBase) are useful prototyping tools. The process of building an event-driven business solution prototype involves the following steps:

1. Build a relational table for each attribute list included in the model.
2. Develop input screens for recording and maintaining processes.
3. Develop queries and report formats for reporting processes.
4. Write individual procedures for each recording, maintaining, and reporting process by translating the Structured English into the database management system application language.
5. Develop a menu hierarchy consisting of four options: record event data, maintain reference data, generate reports, and exit.
6. Link individual procedures to the menu hierarchy. Each information process becomes a sub-item of either the record, maintain, or report main menu choices.

Once the prototype is operational, it should be tested to make sure it satisfies the requirements of the solution. Invariably changes will be required. It is uncanny how businesspeople, like anyone else, are better able to specify their requirements by interacting with a prototype than by looking at models on paper. A prototype brings the requirements to life.

THE INCREDULITY OF MANKIND

At the risk of sounding religious, we have found that buying into the event-driven concepts requires a leap of faith. People often tell us after we have presented these concepts, "It sounds nice, but does it really work?" It seems all of us have a bit of what Machiavelli described as the "incredulity of mankind" in us—we do not truly believe in anything new until we have had actual experience with it.

One alternative, therefore, is to convince you to build a solution and see for yourself. However, unless you feel extremely confident with the material in this chapter we doubt you will be running out to build a solution right away.

Chapter Six

Proof of Concept
This Is Not a Pipe Dream.

HOW DO YOU PROVE THE CONCEPT?

This chapter provides a critical evaluation of the event-driven solution concepts to verify that they are both viable and valuable. To do so, we will concentrate on what event-driven solutions avoid and what they enable. Although we could resort to a lengthy stream of anecdotal evidence for support, we wish to focus our proof on reason rather than rhetoric. Anyone with a concept to sell can provide testimonials to support their claims. We suggest a different approach—establishing criteria for evaluating the value of event-driven solution concepts. By doing so, we intend to elevate the evaluation of event-driven, or any other, proposed solution concepts above the use of late-night TV testimonials.

EVALUATION CRITERIA

We suggest two criteria to guide our evaluation:

First, do event-driven concepts avoid the weaknesses associated with traditional systems? If they do not, at a minimum, address the weaknesses of traditional systems identified in Chapter Two, there is little reason for more analysis. At a minimum, event-driven solutions must overcome the weaknesses of the traditional systems architecture. However, overcoming the weaknesses of traditional systems is a necessary, but not a sufficient condition for proving the viability and value of event-driven solutions.

Second, do event-driven solutions enable organizations to meet present and future challenges? The real value of event-driven solutions rests in how well they step up to the challenges facing organizations today and tomorrow. Specifically, do they facilitate significant and continual improvement in business processes, organization structures, use of IT, and business measurements?

Focusing on these criteria will guide our evaluation of event-driven solutions and provide some measure of proof as to their viability and value. Furthermore, these criteria set a new standard for evaluating any proposed solution.

ARE THE WEAKNESSES OF THE TRADITIONAL ARCHITECTURE RESOLVED?

In Chapter Two we identified and explained the nature of eight fundamental weaknesses of traditional systems. We concluded that these weaknesses result in a dysfunctional technical and organizational architecture. Therefore, we will use each of the eight weaknesses as criteria for evaluating event-driven business solutions. If event-driven solutions do not overcome these eight fundamental weaknesses, we can conclude they will be equally dysfunctional.

Because the first four weaknesses are so closely related, we will address all four at once:

Weaknesses 1–4.   *Stored data has limited characteristics about transactions.*

Data classification schemes are not always appropriate or supportive.

Aggregation level of stored data is too high.

Useful integration of financial and nonfinancial data across the organization is difficult, if not impossible.

Collectively, the first four weaknesses reveal that data in traditional systems are too limited in terms of the dimensions captured, too biased toward a single view of the business, and too aggregated to support the varying degrees of detail requested by information customers across the organization. The traditional architecture attempts to integrate a variety of business data by navigating through a network of system interfaces. However, without addressing the first three weaknesses, the data in traditional functional systems are poorly integrated, particularly the financial and nonfinancial data. Not only are there weaknesses in the data that are captured, data about some business events may not be captured at all.

Some have suggested that the cure to this problem is developing a data warehouse that integrates the data stored in the traditional functional applications (e.g., marketing, accounts payable, accounts receivable, payroll, cost accounting, or production). Attempting to integrate functional data this way assumes that functional data does not have the first three weaknesses and that integration can be achieved after the fact. However, traditional systems often have significant gaps and overlaps in the data from the start. Attempting to subsequently integrate the data using some kind of executive information system that can pull data from a host of feeder systems is an attempt to substitute providing a single point of access to the data for data integration. It does not solve the underlying problems of limited dimensions, bias, aggregation, and detail-level integration.

A limited degree of integration may be achieved with a financial data warehouse, but attempting to integrate functional data to support the development of an enterprise data warehouse having both financial and nonfinancial views has thus far proven to be a pipe dream. *You cannot integrate that which is not integrated from the beginning.* Doing so is akin to the Mother Goose story of Humpty Dumpty. No matter how many horses and how many soldiers (accounting and IT professionals), Humpty Dumpty and nonintegrated transaction data will never be put back together again. Solving the integration problem requires that the first three weaknesses be addressed first. It has been demonstrated repeatedly that technology cannot integrate that which is not integrated conceptually in the first place.

Do event-driven business solutions overcome these fundamental weaknesses? Absolutely. To substantiate this we will use the mail order example discussed in Chapter Five as the context for our discussion (see Figure 6–1 and 6–2). From the list of attributes associated with the REAL business

FIGURE 6-1
Mail-Order Sales/Collection Process Solution Context Diagram

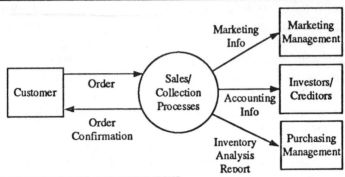

DATA/INFORMATION FLOW DESCRIPTIONS

Order = Time + Customer-Name + Customer-Address + Phone + Ship-to-Information + {Item + Qty}
Order-Confirmation = Confirmation# + Customer-Name + Customer-Address + Phone + {Item# + Item-
    Description + Qty-Ordered + Order-Price} + Ship-to-Info + Subtotal + Tax +
    Total-Order-Amount
Marketing-Info = (Product-Margin-Report, Product-Catalogue, Salesperson-Performance-Report)
Product-Margin-Report = Report-Date + {Item# + Units-Sold + $Volume + Unit-Margin }+
    Total-Units-Sold + Total-$Volume + Avg-Unit-Margin
Salesperson-Performance-Report = Report-Date + {Salesperson-ID + Name + Commission-Rate +
    Units-Sold + $Volume + Avg-Unit-Margin}
Product-Catalogue = Item# + Description + Color + Size + Current-Price + Current-Cost
Accounting-Info = Revenue + Cost-of-Goods-Sold + Gross-Margin + Accounts-Receivable
Inventory-Analysis-Report = Report-Date + {Item# + Units-Sold + Units-On-Hand + Units-on-Order}

---

process model it is fairly obvious that multidimensional characteristics are captured for each transaction. The data can provide answers to the essential questions outlined in Chapter Three about events (e.g., what happened and when, what was involved, who was involved, and where it happened?).

Furthermore, the events included in the mail-order model are not limited to a narrow functional focus involving a limited set of transactions of the overall business process. The mail-order model includes all events within the business process which management has chosen to plan, control, and evaluate. None of the essential aspects of the process are arbitrarily excluded due to organizational boundaries or parochial thinking. The model includes data which generally resides in at least four different systems in a traditional architecture (e.g., order entry system, warehouse system, cash receipts system, and accounts receivable system).

The mail order example also demonstrates how data are stored without a particular classification bias (e.g., a chart of accounts). Only the raw details

FIGURE 6-2
Mail-Order Sales/Collection REAL Business Process Model

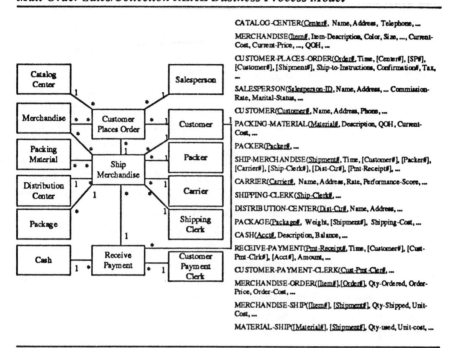

CATALOG-CENTER(Center#, Name, Address, Telephone, ...

MERCHANDISE(Item#, Item-Description, Color, Size, ..., Current-Cost, Current-Price, ..., QOH, ...

CUSTOMER-PLACES-ORDER(Order#, Time, [Center#], [SP#], [Customer#], [Shipment#], Ship-to-Instructions, Confirmation#, Tax, ...

SALESPERSON(Salesperson-ID, Name, Address, ... Commission-Rate, Marital-Status, ...

CUSTOMER(Customer#, Name, Address, Phone, ...

PACKING-MATERIAL(Material#, Description, QOH, Current-Cost, ...

PACKER(Packer#, ...

SHIP-MERCHANDISE(Shipment#, Time, [Customer#], [Packer#], [Carrier#], [Ship-Clerk#], [Dist-Ctr#], [Pmt-Receipt#], ...

CARRIER(Carrier#, Name, Address, Rate, Performance-Score, ...

SHIPPING-CLERK(Ship-Clerk#, ...

DISTRIBUTION-CENTER(Dist-Ctr#, Name, Address, ...

PACKAGE(Package#, Weight, [Shipment#], Shipping-Cost, ...

CASH(Acct#, Description, Balance, ...

RECEIVE-PAYMENT(Pmt-Receipt#, Time, [Customer#], [Cust-Pmt-Clrk#], [Acct#], Amount, ...

CUSTOMER-PAYMENT-CLERK(Cus-Pmt-Clerk#, ...

MERCHANDISE-ORDER([Item#],[Order#], Qty-Ordered, Order-Price, Order-Cost, ...

MERCHANDISE-SHIP([Item#], [Shipment#], Qty-Shipped, Unit-Cost, ...

MATERIAL-SHIP([Material#], [Shipment#], Qty-used, Unit-cost, ...

describing the essential characteristics of the business process are included in the attribute lists. Arbitrary aggregations such as quantity of products sold, total monthly sales, or amount of cash collected from customers are also avoided so as to not preclude the wide variety of details that could be captured about business events.

Lastly, the model illustrates how all aspects of the data are integrated into one description of the business process. There are no separations between financial and nonfinancial or any other type of data. One cohesive picture of the business process supports both financial and nonfinancial views.

Addressing the data-related weaknesses also simplifies what have appeared to be complex processing problems. Let's turn our attention to the process-related weaknesses of traditional systems.

Weakness 5.   *The way data is recorded and maintained seriously limits the system's ability to provide timely support for decision makers.*

Timeliness problems in traditional systems are primarily due to record-
ing multiple copies of the business data in separate systems for each
information customer view. Generally, data are reprocessed to create various
views that cannot be generated by any other system. Once all customer views
can be generated from one integrated store of business data, the need for
recording and maintaining the data in separate systems disappears.

By eliminating multiple recording processes, we eliminate the arbitrary
delays and time based discrepancies resulting from data flowing from one
system to another before it is ready for use by information customers. Using
the event-driven approach, there is no reason to rerecord data once all the
essential aspects of the resources, events, agents, and locations are captured.
Any recording redundancy unnecessarily delays the availability of the data
and results in duplicate descriptions of the business which must be periodically reconciled—a costly, and cumbersome approach.

Conceptually, once the data are recorded, they are available for use. For
many organizations with events occurring all over the globe, a country, a
region, or even a plant, having timely access to data is partly dependent on
having a telecommunications infrastructure that allows timely availability of
data throughout the organization once it is captured.

Although most organizations still do not have a global communications
infrastructure that supports instantaneous data availability, new technologies
are making this more and more a reality every day. The important point is that
as telecommunications capabilities increase, instantaneous availability of
business data will become more and more feasible and will approach what is
conceptually possible with event-driven solutions—real-time reporting—
just like in an F-15!

Weakness 6.   *Traditional processing methods are not very adap-*
                     tive to changing business requirements.

Throughout this book we have continually referred to the pervasive
changes occurring in organizations and society at large. Two characteristics
of traditional systems contribute to their inability to respond to changing
business requirements. First, they are at best loosely linked with the underlying business processes. Second, the fragile nature of traditional system's
architecture makes it difficult to respond to changes in information reporting
requirements which are the most common requirement changes.

Although underlying business processes do change and result in the need to change solution requirements, most solution requirement changes involve changes in information, not business, processes (what and how data are recorded, maintained, and reported). The traditional systems architecture addresses these changes by prescribing the need for a new system to meet each new information processing requirement. Responding to changing requirements is made difficult because the system architecture is not linked to the underlying business processes.

Event-driven business solutions adapt easily to changing requirements by being inherently linked to the underlying business process. Unlike traditional systems, event-driven solutions are defined by, and help define business processes. Changing the business process is equivalent to changing the solution, and vice versa. Later in this chapter we will show that this tight link results in capturing the essential data describing business events which can easily adapt to, and even anticipate, changing reporting requirements. Also, we will discuss how event-driven solutions enable organizations to meet changing business requirements.

Weakness 7.   *Implementing and maintaining internal controls are costly, ineffective, and not performed in a timely manner.*

Efforts to control risk with traditional systems are typically an afterthought or arbitrarily divided. When controlling risk is an afterthought, the organization is vulnerable to significant loss or damage. When the responsibility to control risk is divided, efforts to control risk are unnecessarily costly. Either approach is undesirable. The primary reason for this state of affairs is the complexity of the traditional systems architecture and the way the architecture relegates concern over control primarily to financial systems.

The event-driven architecture facilitates controlling risk by simplifying the technical architecture, making controls over risk an essential part of solution requirements, and integrating responsibility to control risk. The simplification of the technical architecture alone greatly simplifies the task of controlling risk. For example, having one integrated store of data will completely eliminate the need to reconcile data among traditional systems. Because data are only recorded once, any controls over data entry can be integrated with one recording process and applied to every business event.

Furthermore, instead of focusing most control efforts only on the financial system, the control focus can be directly applied to all the organization's business and information processes.

We will spend more time on the issue of controlling risk later. For now, we simply want to emphasize that the event-driven architecture avoids the weaknesses in traditional systems and enables an organization to more aggressively control risk.

Weakness 8.   *Antiquated processing and storage methods are costly to maintain and operate.*

Every system costs money. The problem with traditional systems, however, is that they are unnecessarily costly. The primary reason is the duplication in data, processing, and personnel involved in defining, developing, operating, and evaluating solutions.

By simplifying the architecture we can significantly reduce the amount of technological and human resources required to store and process business data and rules. We have already mentioned a few examples in which organizations have realized tremendous savings by implementing event-driven solutions. However, simply contrasting the two architectures makes it fairly obvious that substantial savings can be realized. Each of the following are straightforward examples of savings:

Recording processes. Because data are integrated, only one recording process is maintained and executed for each business event. Data need not be rerecorded in multiple systems.

Storage and processing hardware. Because of the tremendous storage and processing redundancy in traditional systems, less hardware and processing resources are actually needed overall by integrating storage and processing requirements into one solution.

Technical personnel. By eliminating storage and processing redundancies, redundancies in technical personnel are eliminated as well. The need for so many accounting and IT professionals decreases substantially. These skills can thereby be redirected to solving business problems instead of maintaining an unnecessarily expensive and cumbersome technical architecture and measurement system.

These are not trivial savings! These savings result in increases directly to an organization's bottom line.
Avoiding the eight weaknesses of traditional systems architecture is quite an accomplishment. However, this is not enough. The question remaining is whether event-driven solutions enable organizations to step up to the challenges of today's business environment. To face today's challenges, event-driven solutions must demonstrate their ability to facilitate an immediate, significant breakthrough in:

Business processes.

Organization structures.

Uses of IT.

Business measurements.

By showing how event-driven solutions address these challenges, we will be doing two things. First, we will demonstrate how event-driven solutions do more than simply address the weaknesses of traditional systems. Second, we will set a new standard by which any proposed solution concepts are measured. Our immediate attention will focus on business measurements and how they support the decision making process.

FACILITATE CONTINUAL IMPROVEMENT IN DECISION SUPPORT

To start our discussion of improving decision support, let's review the basic nature of the decision making process (see Figure 6–3). The need to make a decision is driven by a problem or opportunity facing a decision maker who must make a choice. If the result of the choice is not terribly important the decision maker may leave the choice to chance. Assuming, however, the choice is important, useful information is needed to help choose among alternative solutions and opportunities. Information is utilized to guide the decision process. We typically assume that better information plus better decision processes will invariably result in a better choices.

Better information + Better decision process = Better choice

FIGURE 6-3
Basic Decision Process

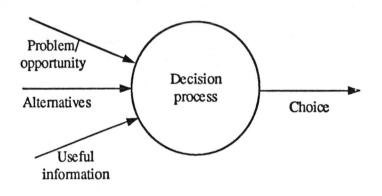

With this common sense model of decision making in mind, we have at least three methods by which we can improve decision making:

Provide better information.

Improve the decision process.

Automate the decision process.

For now, we will focus on providing better information and leave improving or automating the decision process to others. By improving the quality of information available for decision makers we directly contribute to improving the quality of decision making and enable efforts to improve and even automate decision processes as well.

Before showing how event-driven solutions can provide better information, we will illustrate the development of traditional reports. As a basis for our discussion we will use the models of the mail-order sales/collection process (see Figure 6–1 and 6–2). The mail-order sales/collection solution context identifies a variety of fairly traditional forms of both financial and nonfinancial output.

An Order-Confirmation report on the context diagram is an example of traditional information. Generating this information involves locating each element of the output (e.g., Order-Confirmation) in the attribute lists, applying rules to select the appropriate occurrences of the attribute, then applying rules for transforming the attribute read into the output element desired. For example, generating the Confirmation#, Customer-Name, Customer-Address, Phone, and Ship-to-Info simply involves selecting the right occurrences from the CUSTOMER-PLACES-ORDER and CUSTOMER attribute lists that are related to a specific Order #. Generating the Item#, Item-Description, Qty-Ordered, and Order-Price involves selecting the related occurrences from both the MERCHANDISE and MERCHANDISE-ORDER attribute lists and then grouping the information for display.

The remaining elements of the Order-Confirmation are derived using the attribute lists. The Subtotal is derived by summing the product of Qty-Ordered and Order-Price for each item of the order. The Tax is derived by applying a rule (e.g., Tax = Subtotal * 6%) to the Subtotal amount. Finally, Total-Order-Amount is derived by applying yet another rule (Total-Order-Amount = Subtotal + Tax). Figure 6-4 summarizes the process of generating an order confirmation.

FIGURE 6-4
Generating Order-Confirmation from Attribute Lists

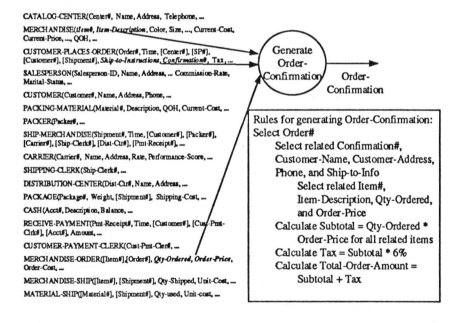

This same type of process can be applied to produce other outputs like the Product-Margin-Report, the Product-Catalogue, or the Salesperson-Performance-Report. Each of these reports involves selecting the appropriate attributes and applying appropriate rules to transform the attributes selected into the output elements.

Generating accounting information follows a similar process. Suppose we want to calculate revenue while preparing an income statement. We must first decide at what point in the sales/collection process revenue is to be recognized. We have three candidates: at the time of order, at the time of shipment, or at the time cash is received. All three are legitimate bases for calculating revenue depending on the information customer. For example, salespeople may recognize revenue at the time of the order; stockholders, governmental agencies (domestic or foreign), or executive management may recognize revenue at the time of shipment; and taxing authorities may recognize revenue at the time payment is received.

Which view is right? All three! Again, each information customer is the final arbiter of what is useful information. However, do we need three different systems to record, maintain, and report each revenue figure? No. We simply need three different sets of rules to report the revenue for each information customer. For example, to report revenue at the Customer-Places-Order event in the sales/collection process, we simply need to apply the rule Revenue = Qty-Ordered * Order-Price for all orders within a time period. Similar rules could be used for reporting revenue at the point of shipment, or when cash is received from the customer. There is no need for three different accounting systems for managerial, financial, and tax reporting purposes, only three different rules for calculating the different figures using the raw event data.

Developing an accounts receivable view is equally straightforward. From an event-driven perspective, accounts receivable is simply the difference between revenue recognized and cash received from customers. If the point of revenue recognition is Cash Receipts, then from an accounting standpoint there are no accounts receivable. However, if revenue is recognized at the time of order or shipment, then accounts receivable must be recognized.

With this view of accounts receivable in mind, generating accounts receivable information is fairly straightforward. First, calculate revenue; second, calculate the related cash receipts; third, take the difference between revenue and cash receipts. This is not a complicated process, and certainly not one that requires recording revenue and cash receipts data again in a separate system simply to take the difference between the two. Accounts receivable is another view of the sales/collection process.

This same logic could be used to generate any other financial statement line item such as Cash, Inventory, Accounts Payable, or Capital Equipment. The point of this explanation is that *once we have captured the essential aspects of the business process any traditional accounting measurement can be generated without recording a subset of the event data in a separate accounting general ledger.*[1] The financial statements are simply one more, albeit a very important, view of the business. There is no reason to have a separate accounting system once the event-driven concepts are applied.

Focusing on capturing essential data describing business events allows us to satisfy a variety of seemingly competing accounting requirements. For example, event-driven solutions have the inherent capability of providing both cash-basis and accrual-basis output from the same data. Why? Because cash and accrual bases are simply two different views of the same underlying business process. One basis recognizes revenue at the time of cash receipts (cash basis), the other at the time of an order or shipment (accrual).

Event-driven solutions help organizations and governments deal with multinational or specialized government reporting requirements as well. Many multinational organizations or organizations in specific industries are required to maintain separate systems to satisfy diverse national, regional, and industry specific reporting requirements. Once the essential characteristics of the underlying business events have been captured, any number of reporting requirements can be satisfied using the single collection of business data. Although reporting requirements may vary widely, the nature of business event data does not. This is a particularly attractive feature of event-driven solutions given the movement underway toward globalization of organizations and economies. For example, emerging free market economies such as Russia that have drastically different reporting requirements can satisfy their own as well as western reporting requirements from a single system. Another example would be the unique and frequently changing requirements for natural gas pipeline companies in the U.S. that must report to the Federal Energy Regulatory Commission.

---

[1]For a detailed description of materializing financial accounting statements from an event-driven solution see E.L. Denna, and W.E. McCarthy, "An Events Accounting Foundation for DSS Implementation," *Decision Support Systems: Theory and Application*, Edited by C.W. Holsapple and A.B. Winston (Berlin: Springer-Verlag, 1987).

tom-line is that event-driven solutions eliminate the need for _____ disclosure requirements. Any number of disclosure requirements can be satisfied from the event-driven solution without compromising any one view.

So much for generating traditional information. Now the question is, What can we do to provide better information? Some have confused providing better information with defining the optimal view of a business to satisfy all decision maker requirements. As you can imagine, these efforts result in either broad concepts that are difficult to apply to specific situations, or in narrow implementations that cannot be generalized. Academicians have refined both extremes to a science.

Attempting to provide one final definition of useful information is complicated by at least two factors:

First, everyone approaches decision making differently. Individual and group perceptions vary as to what constitutes better information. Therefore, each information customer appropriately has a different definition of better information based upon their own experiences, biases, and opportunities.

Second, individual and group perceptions (both inside and outside the organization) of useful information will change. As problems, opportunities, and alternatives facing decision makers change, so will the information they consider useful and valuable.

Traditional systems architectures have attempted to satisfy the different views by building separate systems for each individual or group view. When faced with limited time, money, and talented people, only a limited number of these systems and views can be developed and supported. Therefore, a few "important" or politically prominent views end up being supported (e.g., accounting) while other less important information customers (e.g., operations and management) go without.

Event-driven solutions provide a complete set of disaggregated data, containing both financial and nonfinancial measures, and let each information customer select and format which is relevant to their decision. Because of the nature of event-driven data, exploration can proceed in a variety of directions. For example, information customers can look at:

Any events of a business process by time, agents, resources, and locations.

Any period of time by events, agents, resources, and locations.

Resources by type of event, time, agents, and locations.

Agents by type of event, time, resources, and locations.

Locations by type of event, time, agents, and resources.

Once the issue of data availability is resolved, the usefulness and value of the event-driven data is dependent on the time and imagination each information customer wants to apply to exploring the data. The greater the time and imagination applied, the greater the value of the event-driven solution data. Event-driven solutions create a whole new world for decision making by:

Reducing the uncertainty involved in decision making. Instead of having fragmented and incompatible pictures of business processes as in traditional systems, event-driven solutions present a cohesive picture of the essential aspects of business processes.

Adapting to decision maker individuality. Event-driven solutions avoid prescribing specific views of the data. Instead, each information customer is free to select whatever data they are authorized to view and apply whatever rules they feel appropriate to transform the data into useful information.

Providing a platform for improving and automating decision processes. Because event-driven solutions remove uncertainty about the details of business processes, information customers can refine their decision processes. Furthermore, once a reliable decision making process is developed, the process can be automated and take advantage of the event-driven solution data without human intervention.

In summary, event-driven solutions facilitate initially dramatic, and, thereafter, continuous improvement in decision support by providing a rich information resource and enabling decision processes to be improved and even automated.

FACILITATE CONTINUAL IMPROVEMENT IN BUSINESS AND INFORMATION PROCESSES

To respond to new challenges, organizations must constantly improve business and information processes. The essence of process improvement focuses on:

Eliminating nonessential characteristics of processes.

Automating essential characteristics of processes.

Enabling new essential aspects of processes.

The essential aspects of business processes include its resources, events, agents, locations, and rules. Therefore, changing the essence of business processes involves adding, deleting, or modifying its resources, events, agents, locations, and rules. Any change in an underlying business process must also be reflected in the related information processes. The essential aspects of information processes include:

The data that are recorded and maintained.

The information that is reported.

The rules governing the recording, maintaining, and reporting processes.

The major problem with traditional systems is that even the most subtle changes in the business process can result in a need for wholesale changes in the information processes. However, because event-driven solutions are defined by the essential characteristics of business processes, any changes in the essence of the organization can be handled in a straightforward manner. Remember, it all comes down to data and process. Therefore, changes result in any one or more of the following:

Adding, deleting, or modifying data to be recorded and maintained.

Adding, deleting, or modifying types of information to be reported.

Adding, deleting, or modifying the rules of the recording, maintaining, and reporting processes.

We demonstrated how each of these changes is handled in Chapter Five while discussing the nature of event-driven business solution requirements. Responding to changing requirements requires one or more of the following:

Adding, deleting, or modifying data stores representing a process's resources, events, agents, and locations.

Adding, deleting, or modifying business process rules.

Adding, deleting, or modifying the recording, maintaining, and reporting processing rules.

These isolated changes stand in stark contrast to the changes required in traditional architectures when each change can have a significant ripple effect on many other up- and down-stream applications.

FACILITATE CONTINUAL IMPROVEMENT IN ORGANIZATIONAL STRUCTURE

Organizations exist to convert goods and services acquired into goods and services for customers (see Figure 6–5). Organizations have three basic processes: acquiring needed goods and services, converting goods and

FIGURE 6-5
The Purpose of an Organization

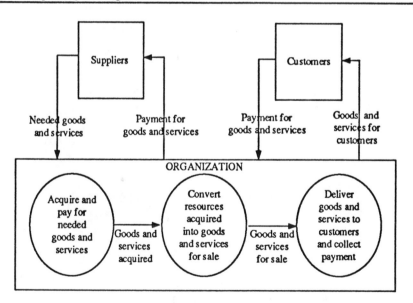

services acquired into goods and services for sale, and delivering the goods and services to customers and collecting payment. This model applies to both profit and nonprofit organizations.

The purpose of an organization's structure is to see that its business processes are properly managed. Management responsibilities include defining, developing, executing, and evaluating processes and their solutions. Each member of an organization is given a stewardship for one or more of the four management responsibilities. The scope of these responsibilities can be for a single event, more than one event, for an entire process, or several organization processes. Each organization member must also report to someone responsible for evaluating their performance. Individual stewardships and reporting responsibilities define the essential nature of an organization's structure.

The nature of organization structures varies widely. At the extremes, organizations can have everything from the rigid hierarchies of yesteryears to a loose confederation of problem-driven project teams (see Figure 6–6). So

FIGURE 6-6
Extremes of Organization Structures

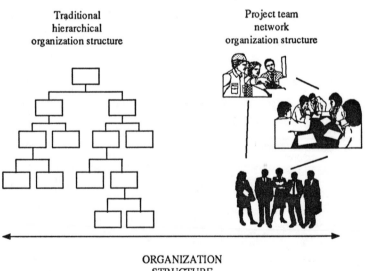

Traditional
hierarchical
organization structure

Project team
network
organization structure

ORGANIZATION
STRUCTURE
CONTINUUM

which is the best structure?

which extreme is right? The answer depends on a variety of factors ranging from the particular culture of the organization to its environment, regulations, and the talents of its members. Most organizations today are becoming an amalgam of various structures that are attempting to adapt to the challenges shaping the organization's purpose and value. However, such fluid, dynamic organization structures drive traditional systems development and maintenance personnel absolutely bananas because these people know more about organization boundaries (e.g., marketing, accounting, accounts payable, purchasing, and receiving) and politics, than business processes.

Event-driven business solutions make two significant contributions toward adapting IT use to a fluid organization structure. First, event-driven solutions are inherently independent of organization structure. Event-driven solutions model the business process underlying any current and potential organization structure. Therefore, structure can be changed without worrying about its impact on the solution.

Second, event-driven solutions provide a clear picture of an organization's essential business processes as well as its essential stewardships and roles. This serves as a litmus test by which current roles and responsibilities can be evaluated. Often, event-driven analysis reveals situations within an organization in which management of specific business events is either inadequate or redundant, neither of which is desirable.

As a result, event-driven solutions impact organization structure by:

① **Reducing the number of people needed to run the business.** Once the essence of the business process is identified, management redundancy can be eliminated. Because so many organization structures today are redundant in assigning and supervising responsibility to define, develop, execute, and evaluate business processes, fewer people are needed after implementing an event-driven solution, particularly in traditional administrative positions. Therefore, implementing event-driven solutions can result in tremendous staff reductions or reallocations.

② **Enabling individuals and organization structures to become** more fluid. As resources, events, agents/roles, locations, and rules change so does the structure of the organization. Therefore, instead of someone pointing to a multilevel organization chart to identify what they do, they point to a business event or process and say, "That's what I do." The next day, who they report to or what they do may be completely different.

Involving everyone in all aspects of business process management. The flip side of not needing as many people who can only participate in one managerial duty is that event-driven solutions trigger the demand for multidimensional people who can participate in all aspects of managing business processes. The buzz word typically attributed to this kind of a transformation is "employee empowerment." The event-driven organization helps identify what employees are empowered to do—solve problems by defining, developing, executing, and evaluating business processes and their solutions.

So how do you make this all work? Here are a few keys to success:

Make sure someone is responsible for each business event. Too often, individual business events within processes are either co-managed, over-managed, or not managed at all. Therefore, once a business process is identified some individual should be given responsibility to coordinate efforts to define, develop, execute, and evaluate the process.

Get everyone involved in all aspects of management responsibilities. Everyone can and should contribute in efforts to define, develop, execute, and evaluate business processes and their solutions. When people are arbitrarily excluded from any of the four management responsibilities, tremendous insights and synergy are unnecessarily lost: an unfortunate and unnecessary state of affairs for any organization today.

Keep management layers to a minimum. Because everyone can be involved in management responsibilities, very few management layers are needed. Many organizations find they can operate with as little as three layers of management: line personnel with responsibility to manage individual events, managers with the responsibility to manage entire processes, and executives with the responsibility to manage across all organization processes.

Many are calling for very different organization structures. Tom Peters suggests that organizations be involved in, "constant reorganization, in the sense of perpetual reconfiguration of project team structures and network structure."[2] Most accounting and IT professionals react negatively to such

---

[2] T. Peters, *Liberation Management:Necessary Disorganization for the Nanosecond Nineties*, (New York: Alfred A. Knopf, 1992), p. 155.

ideas because of the work required to change traditional systems to adapt to changes in organization structure. The typical reaction to such ideas is, "How in the world . . . ? If management would simply make up their mind we could finally . . ." Most of this reaction to fluid organization structures is directly attributable to being mired in traditional system and organizational concepts. Event-driven solution concepts can significantly reduce resistance to changing organization structures.

FACILITATE CONTINUAL IMPROVEMENT IN CONTROLS OVER BUSINESS AND INFORMATION PROCESS RISK

Because changes are required in the nature of business processes, organization structures, and the way we use information technology, we should not be surprised that changes are needed in the way we control risk. Traditional efforts to control risk typically involve either making a token effort to appease regulators, investors, or creditors, or isolating responsibility for controls to auditors. If the organization is large enough, it may develop an internal audit staff. Otherwise, it will rely on external audit professionals. Making a token effort to control risk, or isolating responsibility to auditors is an inadequate, costly, and unnecessary approach. A change is needed!

Aside from enabling a change in philosophy regarding control as we discussed in Chapter Four, event-driven solutions facilitate continual improvement in controlling risk by:

Reducing the cost of controlling risk. This is due primarily to eliminating the need for duplicate systems and their associated resource requirements.

Simplifying the task of controlling risk. This is due to clearly identifying the types and nature of risk: business process risk, information processing risk, and technological risk (see Chapter Four).

Focusing efforts to control risk. By reducing the cost and simplifying the task of controlling risk, organizations can better focus available resources on the task of controlling risk.

Making controlling risk an integral part of defining, developing, executing, and evaluating business solutions. Instead of controls being a primary feature of only the accounting system, they become an integral part of every event-driven solution.

Involving everyone in controlling risk. As controlling risk becomes an integral part of solution development, all organization personnel become directly involved in controlling risk.

Although event-driven solutions facilitate improvement in controls, some may express concern that event-driven solutions violate principles established by the audit profession. Much of the traditional control philosophy is embodied in Statement of Auditing Standards No. 55 (SAS 55). This standard identifies three aspects of an organization's control structure: the control environment, the accounting system, and the control procedures (see Figure 6–7). The big question to answer with respect to SAS 55 is whether event-driven solutions in some way violate any of the traditional concepts of internal control.

FIGURE 6-7
Traditional Organization Control Structure

Traditional Internal Control Structure

Control Environment Subelements of control environment	Accounting System Objectives that must be satisfied	Control Procedures Categories of control procedures
- Management philosophy and operating style. - Organizational structure. - Audit committee. - Methods to communicate the assignment of authority and responsibility. - Management control methods. - Internal audit function. - Personnel policies and procedures. - External influences.	- Validity. - Authorization. - Completeness. - Valuation. - Classification. - Timing. - Posting and summarization.	- Adequate separation of duties. - Proper authorization of transactions and activities. - Adequate documents and records. - Physical control over assets and records. - Independent checks on performance.

The Control Environment

A strong control environment requires, among other things, employee responsibility and commitment, an internal audit function, and an audit committee. Event-driven solutions in no way preclude an organization from having any of the elements of a strong control environment. Nor do they prescribe a certain management philosophy, operating style, organization structure, or personnel policies and procedures. Instead, they strengthen an organization's ability to communicate the assignment of authority and responsibility and management's control methods by embedding controls directly into the solution. Therefore, using the solution means executing management controls—one cannot be done without the other. As a result, management is better able to respond to external influences that tend to increase their exposure to risk (e.g., where they operate, the roles and responsibilities performed by personnel, and the resources involved).

The Accounting System

The objectives of the accounting system focus on the integrity of the data that are recorded and the information that is reported. Although event-driven solutions eliminate the need for a separate accounting system, they still can be used to achieve the objectives prescribed in SAS 55. With event-driven solutions, all the appropriate controls insuring the validity and completeness of recorded data can be performed in real-time while the event occurs. Data need not be rerecorded in a separate accounting system. This eliminates the possibility of errors which would compromise the validity and completeness of the data available for reporting purposes. Recording data in real-time also addresses at least part of the timing issue—there is no difference between when the event occurs and when the event data is recorded.

When information is derived directly from the recorded data, appropriate rules must be executed to ensure the right data are properly summarized, classified, and valued according to each information customer's rules. This includes selecting the data appropriate to a particular window of time. This is a reporting issue, not an issue of trying to decide which debits and credits to record.

One last thing regarding the objectives of accounting systems. As illustrated earlier, accounting numbers can be derived directly from the raw event data. Therefore, because of the architecture of event-driven solutions, there is no need to worry about posting procedures. Posting is a carryover from the manual bookkeeping procedures and is unnecessary in event-driven solutions.

Control Procedures

As we have already explained, *proper event authorization and documentation becomes an integral part of the event-driven solution.* Authorization and documentation procedures are executed in real time rather than when data hits an accounting system. Therefore, procedures are applied to all business events, not just a statistical sample of the subset of events (accounting transactions) traditionally affecting the accounting system. Furthermore, because control procedures are a part of the solution itself, the solution becomes a participant in the separation of duties by performing the recording responsibility. This provides efficiencies for the organization by reducing the dependence on human information processing and its inevitable errors and irregularities.

Event-driven solutions shift the concern regarding physical control over records to one of obtaining access to the solution and its processes. Therefore, dependence on control procedures dealing with manual processing environments is replaced by dependence on information technology itself. This is somewhat disconcerting to some auditors who do not have an adequate understanding of or appreciation for IT. In such cases, the temptation may be to introduce control procedures used in manual processing environments (e.g., save printed copies of event documentation instead of duplicate electronic copies, require handwritten instead electronic signatures, or restrict access to IT specialists instead of making it available to all organization employees). Paranoia born of IT ignorance results in costly and largely ineffective control procedures.

Event-driven solutions provide a large contribution to providing independent checks on individual and organization performance. We have already mentioned one contribution—every control procedure embedded in the solution is applied to every business event within the scope of the solution. However, this only addresses procedures we use for risk we currently know of and wish to control. It speaks nothing of detecting errors and irregularities yet unknown or which are too costly to control in real time. The contribution of event-driven solutions is to enable auditors to be much more aggressive in post period investigations by providing a complete and integrated description of the business process in a timely manner. Instead of spending time trying to integrate data about business processes so they can perform various tests, time is focused on exploring the data looking for undesirable trends that may warn of impending errors and irregularities.

As you can see, event-driven solutions do support a traditional control structure. However, they also facilitate significant improvements in an organization's controls, enabling the organization to respond more effectively and efficiently to the risks it faces. As a result, controlling risk and auditing becomes much more a value-add activity than compliance with regulations and standards.

THE BOTTOM LINE

Needless to say, event-driven solutions are not a pipe dream. They are of tremendous value to organizations attempting to compete in today's world. So, what's the catch?

There are costs. Probably the costs most worth noting include helping people get the vision and defining and implementing the solution requirements. But there are benefits too. Adopting event-driven solution concepts enables organizations to overcome the weaknesses of traditional business processes, organization structures, and uses of IT. The concepts facilitate dramatic and continual improvement in business processes, organization structures, uses of IT, and business measurements. Our experience with a variety of organizations is that the payoff from adopting event-driven concepts is immediate and profound.

You do not have to be a large multinational to be able to muster the resources required to define, develop, execute, and evaluate event-driven solutions or to realize their benefit. Nor do you have to be a small "Ma and Pa" diner to be able to handle the changes in migrating toward event-driven solutions. Each organization will incur unique costs and realize unique benefits, whether a multinational or a small, family-owned upstart company being run out of the back of a pickup truck or a basement. In fact, small companies that adopt these concepts are finding it much easier to grow into big companies because they have a technological architecture that does not need to change as the organization grows.

The key to migrating toward event-driven business solutions is leadership. Leadership requires vision, courage, and an implementation strategy. We hope that we have already provided some vision and courage. Chapter Seven addresses the issue of developing a strategy to implement event-driven solutions.

Chapter Seven

Implementation Implications of Event-Driven Business Solutions
Starting the Revolution!

REALIZING THE EVENT-DRIVEN SOLUTION VISION

The focus throughout the book has been on sharing with you the power of an event-driven business vision. The question left unanswered is how to achieve the vision. To answer this question, let's put event-driven business solutions in perspective and then discuss how they can be implemented (see Figure 7–1).

Business solutions have four components: the underlying business process, the related organization structure, the use of IT, and the related measurements of business results. We have many examples of attempts to solve business problems by not addressing all four of the components (e.g., restructuring the organization, changing the technology utilized, changing the measurements, or even changing the underlying process). These efforts typically fail entirely or have limited success. Solving business problems, therefore, requires attention to all four components.

The four solution components are closely interrelated. Changes in one component can have a significant influence on another. For example, business processes define the essential stewardships of an organization. Therefore, as the nature of a business process changes, so does the stewardships of the organization. Events within a process (and the related stewardships) can be eliminated, automated, or added. Therefore, the nature of the organization structure must also change to properly supervise and coordinate the process's

FIGURE 7-1

The Business Solution Perspective

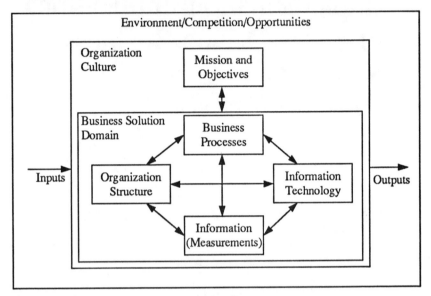

Event-driven business solutions enable continual improvement in business processes, organization structure, information (measurements), and information technology.

stewardships. Furthermore, changes in the underlying business process can affect the use of IT and the process measurements.

Although each solution component has an effect on other components, the impact of business processes on the other components is clearly the most significant. Without a clear definition of the underlying business process, we have no basis for defining the other three components of a solution. Until recently, we have lacked a theory of the nature of business processes.

The contribution of event-driven concepts toward the development of business solutions is their emphasis on the role of the business process in solving business problems and providing a theory of what a business process is. In Chapter Three we described a model of business events and processes. A business event is any process that management wants to plan, control, and evaluate. The model consists of four conceptual objects that are interrelated: an event, resources, agents, and locations. These concepts provide a fairly straightforward means of identifying and validating the essential nature of business events. When a series of events are combined, they provide a model of the business process. The event-driven business process model serves as a basis for specifying the essential characteristics of the organization's structure, the use of IT, and the nature of the process measurements. Let's use the mail-order sales/collection process model as an example to illustrate how the model of the business process helps specify the other three solution components.

Figure 7–2 shows the event-driven business process model of a mail-order sales/collection process. The model specifies how the various events, agents, resources, and locations are related. This model also serves as a basis for evaluating the organization structure responsible for the process by identifying the essential stewardships involved in the process. In this example we have five agents identified: salesperson, customer, carrier, shipping clerk, and

FIGURE 7-2

Mail-order Sales/Collection Business Process Model

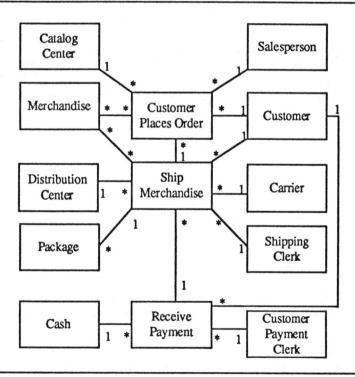

customer payment clerk. Three of the five agents are organization representatives: salesperson, shipping clerk, and customer payment clerk. Therefore, an organization structure must be specified that defines who is to perform each stewardship function and who owns the process.

The model also helps define the use of IT. As described in Chapter Five, three things must be performed using some form of IT:

Record business event data and execute the appropriate business rules.

Maintain resource, agent, and location data.

Generate useful information for information customers.

This results in the architecture shown in Figure 7–3.

FIGURE 7-3
The Event-Driven Solution Architecture

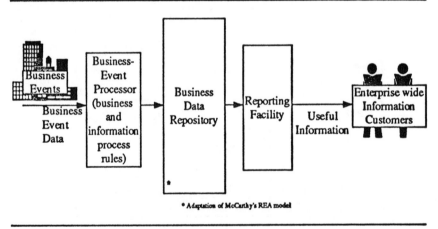

* Adaptation of McCarthy's REA model

In Chapter Five we also described how the model helps define the data to be captured about the business process and how the data serves as a platform to experiment with alternative process measurements (see Figure 7–4). Because the model guides the capture of all essential aspects of the business process it also provides a context for possible measurements. Event-driven solutions provide essential disaggregated data, containing both financial and nonfinancial measures, and let each information customer select the most relevant format for their decision. Because of the nature of event-driven data,

FIGURE 7-4
Mail-order Sales/Collection Process Model With Attribute Lists

REAL Business Process Model

Attribute Lists

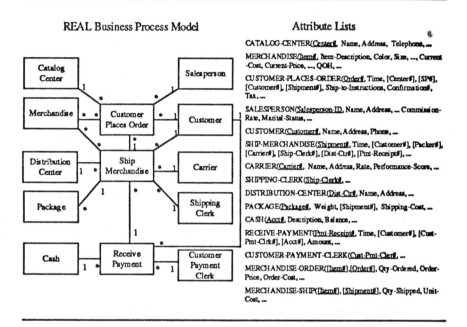

CATALOG-CENTER(Center#, Name, Address, Telephone, ...

MERCHANDISE(Item#, Item-Description, Color, Size, ..., Current-Cost, Current-Price, ..., QOH, ...

CUSTOMER-PLACES-ORDER(Order#, Time, [Center#], [SP#], [Customer#], [Shipment#], Ship-to-Instructions, Confirmation#, Tax, ...

SALESPERSON(Salesperson-ID, Name, Address, ... Commission-Rate, Marital-Status, ...

CUSTOMER(Customer#, Name, Address, Phone, ...

SHIP-MERCHANDISE(Shipment#, Time, [Customer#], [Packer#], [Carrier#], [Ship-Clerk#], [Dist-Ctr#], [Pmt-Receipt#], ...

CARRIER(Carrier#, Name, Address, Rate, Performance-Score, ...

SHIPPING-CLERK(Ship-Clerk#, ...

DISTRIBUTION-CENTER(Dist-Ctr#, Name, Address, ...

PACKAGE(Package#, Weight, [Shipment#], Shipping-Cost, ...

CASH(Acct#, Description, Balance, ...

RECEIVE-PAYMENT(Pmt-Receipt#, Time, [Customer#], [Cust-Pmt-Clrk#], [Acct#], Amount, ...

CUSTOMER-PAYMENT-CLERK(Cust-Pmt-Clerk#, ...

MERCHANDISE-ORDER([Item#],[Order#], Qty-Ordered, Order-Price, Order-Cost, ...

MERCHANDISE-SHIP([Item#], [Shipment#], Qty-Shipped, Unit-Cost, ...

exploration can proceed in a variety of directions. For example, information customers can look at:

Any events of a business process by time, agents, resources, and locations.

Any period of time by events, agents, resources, and locations.

Resources by type of event, time, agents, and locations.

Agents by type of event, time, resources, and locations.

Locations by type of event, time, agents, and resources.

Once the issue of data availability is resolved, the usefulness and value of the event-driven data are dependent on the creativity of each information customer. The greater the creativity the greater the value of the event-driven solution data.

The key to effective business solutions is defining the nature of the underlying business process. Once defined, the process serves as a basis for defining the other solution components. So where does the move toward event-driven business solutions begin? Several steps are important in developing event-driven business solutions (see Figure 7–5).

Clearly Defined Mission, Objectives, and Culture

Implementing event-driven solutions rests upon a clearly defined mission and the corresponding objectives and culture. Business solutions are shaped by the nature of an organization's mission, objectives, and culture which are a response to the organization's environment, competition, and opportunities. However, many organizations go to great lengths to define their mission, objectives, and culture and develop elaborate mission and objectives statements. This information ends up covering the walls of many offices and lobbies. Unfortunately, once this information is distributed, all too often people begin to ask, "OK, now what?" and unfortunately, there is a weak response. Without specifying the critical processes of an organization, the mission and objectives can do more to confuse than clarify.

FIGURE 7-5
The Event-Driven Solution Architecture

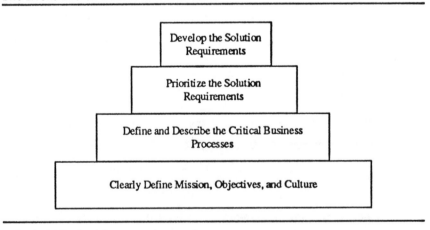

Develop the Solution
Requirements

Prioritize the Solution
Requirements

Define and Describe the Critical Business
Processes

Clearly Define Mission, Objectives, and Culture

Define and Describe the Critical Business Processes

To clearly define a mission and objectives statement, executives must identify the organization's critical processes. Identifying these processes does not grow out of mass interviews of organization members in an effort to find oneself through self-introspection. Defining organization-wide business processes requires an executive level perspective and direction.

Identifying critical business processes is guided by the concepts outlined in Chapter Three regarding the nature of organization processes. At the highest level, every organization has three basic processes: acquire, maintain, and pay for resources; convert resources into goods and services; and, deliver goods and services to customers and collect payment. Each of these processes can be specialized depending on the types of resources, agents, or locations involved. For example, the acquisition/payment process is typically specialized for each of the following resources:

Financing.

Human resources.

Property, plant, and equipment.

Inventories.

Specialized conversion processes depend on the nature of the good or service being produced. We listed several conversion processes in Chapter Three including assembling, growing, excavating, and harvesting. Each process may be specialized depending on the location and agents involved.

Regardless of the degree to which management wishes to specialize, every business process is a special form of the three general processes. These three basic processes provides a powerful model to guide and validate the identification of an organization's business processes. Each critical process represents the need for a solution, which is the next step to consider.

Prioritize, and Plan Solution Projects

Once the critical business processes have been defined by management specific solution development projects must be planned and prioritized. Management shapes the solution projects by defining its mission and objectives, setting solution priorities, assigning a process owner, and dedicating adequate resources to support the development effort.

Planning a solution project involves specifying a clear mission and objectives for the solution team and assigning a process owner and development team. The project should be large enough to solve a meaningful business process but not so large that it becomes unmanageable. A short turn-around time between project approval and project implementation is critical to the overall success of business solutions. Furthermore, each project must be assigned a process owner and a solution development team. The process owner and solution team work hand in hand to develop the solution requirements.

A variety of methods can be used to prioritize projects. These include benchmarking, cost of quality analysis, ROI, cycle time analysis, defect analysis, and so forth. Often, more than one method is used to prioritize the potential solution projects. Regardless of the method used, management must clearly specify the priority of the solution projects to avoid trying to "boil the ocean" by taking on too many solution projects at once.

The solution project mission and objectives should include criteria for measuring the success of the solution project in all four solution components: process, structure, use of IT, and measurements. This provides an objective basis for guiding the development process as well as evaluating the results.

Developing the Solution Requirements

The focus of developing solution requirements should be on defining *what should be*, not what is. The key is to seek input from key organization members that can help define the *desired* nature of the business process and its solution components. Interviews with other organization members should focus more on consensus building than on eliciting solution requirements.

In addition to the suggestions we have mentioned thus far, we have found that success in developing event-driven business solutions is dependent upon three things: executive sponsorship, training and education, and managing change.

EXECUTIVE SPONSORSHIP

Individuals involved in developing event-driven business solutions must posses four critical characteristics: vision, courage, direction, and authority. The first three can be developed by anyone in the organization. However, without someone who has organizationwide authority and support, the chance of the vision being achieved, regardless of the courage and direction, is very low.

Event-driven solution efforts cannot survive without executive-level sponsorship. The reason for this is fairly simple; event-driven business solutions affect all four solution components: process, structure, IT, and measurements. As business processes, organization structures, use of IT, and measurements are challenged, issues are quickly escalated and require executive-level involvement. Without this involvement, solutions will often be sabotaged by those with heavy investments in the old order of things.

Our experience has shown that the support and cooperation of three executives are key to successfully developing event-driven business solutions: the CEO, CFO, and CIO. The reason for the CEO involvement is obvious. The CFO and CIO make two critical contributions. First, both typically have organization-wide perspectives and involvement. Second, each has control over a critical resource: cash and IT. When the CFO and CIO are already organizationally united (typically the CIO reports to the CFO) the only thing lacking is a vision of what event-driven business solutions are all about. With the support of the CEO, work toward fulfilling the event-driven vision can proceed and its successful fulfillment is nearly guaranteed.

TRAINING AND SUPPORT

Although we have tried to provide a clear picture of the nature of event-driven business solutions and how they are developed, we have not intended to provide the detailed training required to actually achieve the vision. At least three types of training are essential.

Executive Level Training and Support

Executive level training and support focuses on transforming mission and objectives statements into a list of prioritized solution development projects. This includes identifying an organization's critical processes, prioritizing the solution projects, identifying process owners, and defining the objectives and measurements of each project.

Event/Process Owner Training and Support

Because event-driven business solutions actually define employee empowerment, they radically alter the traditional responsibilities of organization members. No longer are employees restricted to executing a predefined set of solutions. Instead, event-driven solutions encourage their involvement in, and responsibility for, defining, developing, and evaluating solutions as well.

Although their breadth of responsibility is increased, event/process owners are supported in their efforts to define, develop, execute, and evaluate solutions by solution professionals.

Solution Professional Training and Support

Solution professional training focuses on interviewing and modeling techniques for defining solution requirements. The difficulty in selecting potential solution professionals is that traditional organization structures and education have not addressed the need for such professionals. We have professionals that focus on measurements (accounting), use of IT (IT), or organization structure (organizational behavior), and even processes (process engineers). However, none of these groups have a solutionwide perspective. Therefore, training and support is required to create business solution professionals. Actually, anyone with experience in any one of the solution components can be groomed to become a solution professional. However, without formal training and support, solution professionals do not magically appear.

MANAGING CHANGE AND SHAPING CULTURE

Ignoring change management will bring the best efforts to their knees. Once again, Machiavelli explained:

> It must be considered that there is nothing more difficult to carry out, nor more doubtful of success, nor more dangerous to handle than to initiate a new order of things. For the reformer has enemies in all those who profit by the old order, and only lukewarm defenders by all those who could profit by the new order. This lukewarmness arises partly from fear of their adversaries who have the laws in their favor, and partly from the incredulity of mankind who do not truly believe in anything new until they have had actual experience with it.[1]

The cliche, "There is nothing so constant as change," is as true as it is well-worn. Managing change cannot be trivialized and must be considered while defining, developing, executing, and evaluating new ways of doing things. Although many changes can be anticipated, the task is made more challenging

---

[1]N. Machiavelli, *The Prince*. Translated by Luigi Rice, Rev. E. R. P Vincent (New York: New American Library, 1952) p. 10.

because the impact of changes still catches us by surprise. The world has a way of catching us all by surprise. Changes in political systems, economies, technologies, and societal preferences over the past 10 years alone have provided ample evidence that we will continue to have surprises in our lives. Science fiction writer Isaac Asimov once said:

> it's easier to foresee the automobile than the traffic jam, the atom bomb than nuclear stalemate, the birth control pill than women's liberation. Put another way, the march of technology is inexorable and, to some extent, predictable. But the resulting corporate organizational and managerial ramifications are much harder to imagine.[2]

The tendency is to proceed with a change until it meets with resistance. However, the problem with a reactive posture to managing change and shaping culture is that by the time the negative reaction is exhibited, it is typically too late to do anything about it. It is helpful to understand the impact of change on human behavior, and some principles for managing changes resulting from the development and implementation of event-driven solutions.

Dysfunctional Human Behavior

A commonly asked question is, "Why do people react the way they do to change?" Simply put, people react based upon how the change affects them personally. While some are completely unaffected by changes and events, others are caught in the middle of the storm. When people conclude that a change has a negative effect on them, their behavior can become quite dysfunctional and endanger themselves and the enterprise. Most dysfunctional human behavior is manifested in one or more of three ways:

> *Aggression* involves any attempt by an individual or group to damage the organization or its information system. For example, during the early 1980's, several manufacturers introduced robotics technology into the assembly line. Employees in these organizations saw the robot as a threat to their long-term employment stability. As a result, they did several things to sabotage the move towards robotics. Some employees poured drinks on the computer key-

---

[2]As quoted by R. Carlyle, "The Tomorrow Organization," *Datamation*, Februrary 1, 1990, p. 22.

boards, while others "accidentally" knocked computers off their stands making them crash to the floor, thereby ruining several workstations used to control the robots and driving up the cost of the technology.

Projection involves any effort to blame the system for problems people face. Systems, whether computerized or not, are often blamed for everything from ordering too many items of a particular product to losing an order altogether. You have no doubt had the experience of making a restaurant reservation by telephone and, upon arriving, found they had lost your reservation for your family and 15 friends and relatives. "Our computer must have lost your reservation," is the typical response.

Avoidance involves any attempt to avoid using the system. For example, during the 1980's various large banks became concerned about inconsistencies in the application of loan approval policies across loan officers. Some developed expert system technology to standardize the approval process and assist loan officers in evaluating loan applications. During the development process, however, only a few loan officers were involved. The new system resulted in loan officers becoming little more than glorified data entry clerks. As a result, loan officers avoided the system altogether and reverted back to the old process. The bank eventually pulled the system and made substantial modifications to cater to the preferences of its loan officers although hundreds of thousands of dollars were spent on the system.

Most problems with dysfunctional behavior are spawned by changing current processes, responsibilities, or uses of technology. Properly managing the defining, developing, executing, and evaluating of processes, people, and technology is the key to minimizing dysfunctional behavior on the part of people affected by the changed or the new system.

Principles for Managing Change

Management should consider several issues when contemplating a change. Although some principles are more important than others, none of the following issues should be overlooked or minimized when contemplating a change.

Organization Culture. Each organization has a unique cultu distinguishes it from all others. Changes should support rather than challenge the organization's culture. Proper use of information technology should not presuppose an organization culture or structure. Quite the opposite, the technology allows the organization to choose the culture and structure it desires.

Participation. Before attempting a change, you should carefully analyze the capabilities of those participating in the change process. Organizations with people who are technically weak and largely grounded in traditional ways of thinking and operating must do more planning and creative thinking when instigating a significant change that involves the use of technology than other organizations with strong technological expertise.

Equally important is ensuring widespread representation throughout the organization in the change process. Participants should represent all kinds of organization stewardships and responsibilities. Favoring one type of participant over another can result in significant behavior on the part of those who feel left out or uninformed.

Well Defined Purpose and a Manageable Scope. Few things create greater uncertainty and resistance than not knowing the reason and extent of a change. Once the purpose and scope of the system are identified, management should make every effort to inform all affected parties to prevent any surprises. Minimizing surprises will often minimize resistance to change.

Participant Security and Development. Those who dedicate significant amounts of time and effort to the change process will likely not be as involved in their regular responsibilities. Unless specific assurance is provided to participants regarding their role in the organization most will decline participating or will not give the project their best effort.

Performance Evaluation. Because changes often alter people's responsibilities, changes will likely be required in the way individual performance is measured and evaluated. Without changing the performance evaluation process, changes may obscure personal performance, thus creating disincentives for supporting proposed changes.

Responsibilities for Managing Change

Considering all the factors affecting change, we suggest a division of responsibilities for managing change among management, employees, and IT specialists.

Management should:

Openly support efforts to continually improve all aspects of the organization.

Determine timing for enterprisewide changes.

Approve suggestions for improvement.

Monitor progress of approved changes and insure that measurement systems are adjusted quickly.

Assist in resolving problems resulting from change.

Meanwhile, employees should:

Commit to continual individual and organization improvement.

Actively participate in suggesting and implementing changes.

Demand creative solutions to business and information problems.

Last, solution professionals should:

Understand the impact of IT as a change agent.

Deal with problems in a timely and effective manner.[3]

Following these suggestions increases the likelihood of successfully cultivating a culture of continual improvement and facilitating an organization's efforts to continually improve.

START THE REVOLUTION!

Einstein stated that, "The world will not evolve past its current state of crisis by using the same thinking that created the situation." The "current state of crisis" has been described many ways; the information revolution, the age of the knowledge worker, the death of the industrial organization, the virtual

---

[3]Adapted from P. Flaatten, D. McCubbrey, P. O'Riordan, and K. Burgess, *Foundations of Business Systems* (Chicago: Dryden Press, 1989), p. 42.

corporation, "The Third Wave," "Danger in the Comfort Zone," etc. Much has been written about the changes we are experiencing and their impact on both people and businesses. However, very little has been written to guide you through these changes in a manageable way.

Throughout this book we have focused on giving a vision of how to respond to this new world. This book provides a compass to help you redefine your business and maintain your leadership position by implementing event-driven business solutions. This road map also provides an opportunity for you to participate in establishing a new order of things to remain competitive in today's fast changing world. We invite you to fire the shot heard around your world and start your own revolution.

Index

Also available from Business One Irwin . . .

CASH FLOW AND SECURITY ANALYSIS

Kenneth S. Hackel, President of Systematic Financial Management, Incorporated
Joshua Livnat

This important reference explains, for the first time, what cash flow analysis is all about as it pertains to fundamental security analysis . . . how it differs from accrual accounting . . . and why accounting regulators are gearing investors toward cash flow analysis and away from accrual accounting (with examples of how easy it is to convert). (288 pages)
ISBN: 1-55623-387-6

CORPORATE INFORMATION SYSTEMS MANAGEMENT

The Issues Facing Senior Executives

James I. Cash, Jr., F. Warren McFarlan, and James L. McKenney

The latest edition of this classic guide addresses the leading issues of computer management, identifying ways for you to implement innovative organization, planning, and management control ideas to improve operations efficiency. You will discover valuable strategies to help you meet the challenges posed by expert systems, use information systems to enhance your company's competitive position, master the latest technological advances, and more! (301 pages)
ISBN: 1-55623-615-8

MANAGEMENT INFORMATION SYSTEMS

The Manager's View
Second Edition

Robert Schultheis and Mary Sumner

Through practical, management-oriented problems and cases, as well as through examples of real-life applications, authors Schultheis and Sumner show managers how information technology can be used to support their business strategies. This thoroughly updated guide includes coverage of timely topics such as microcomputer technology; client-server computing; downsizing; executive information systems; multimedia systems; wireless LANs; and much more. (960 pages)
ISBN: 0-256-09366-0

Also available in fine bookstores and libraries everywhere.